T0330314

Inclusive Territories 1

**Territorial Entrepreneurship
and Innovation Set**

coordinated by
Didier Chabaud, Florent Pratlong
and Carlos Moreno

Volume 1

Inclusive Territories 1

Role of Enterprises and Organizations

Edited by

Martine Brasseur
Annie Bartoli
Didier Chabaud
Pascal Grouiez
Gilles Rouet

WILEY

First published 2023 in Great Britain and the United States by ISTE Ltd and John Wiley & Sons, Inc.

ISTE Ltd
27-37 St George's Road
London SW19 4EU
UK

www.iste.co.uk

John Wiley & Sons, Inc.
111 River Street
Hoboken, NJ 07030
USA

www.wiley.com

Library of Congress Control Number: 2023942764

British Library Cataloguing-in-Publication Data
A CIP record for this book is available from the British Library
ISBN 978-1-78630-855-9

Contents

Chapter 3. Contributions of a Science and Technology Park (STP) to Inclusive Mobility for a Territory   45
Isabelle KUSTOSZ and Stéphane MEURIC

Chapter 4. Understanding the Development of Social Enterprise in South Korea   67
Éric BIDET

Introduction

Inclusion in a Territory, Political and Social Issues, Issues for Enterprises

This book is the first in a new set of books launched by ISTE Ltd in partnership with the chair "Entrepreneurship, Territory and Innovation" (ETI) at the IAE Paris Sorbonne Business School directed by Didier Chabaud, Carlos Moreno and Florent Pratlong.

It is part of the "Territory and Inclusion" research program led by CEDAG's "Management, Ethics, Innovation and Society" (MEIS) axis in partnership with the LADYSS Laboratory, the LAREQUOI Center for Research in Management at the Paris-Saclay University in Versailles and the ETI chair at IAE Paris Sorbonne Business School. It questions the links between territory and inclusion with the aim of understanding and characterizing the processes specific to inclusive entrepreneurial ecosystems, as well as identifying the main levers for actions.

In order to explore these themes further, two workshops were organized in 2019 and 2021, bringing together researchers in management sciences, economics and geography, as well as institutional and socio-economic actors. The objective of the first workshop was to clarify the notion of "inclusive territory" while exploring the plurality of entrepreneurial dynamics developed in a territory through the lens of inclusion. A few milestones were thus established. The inclusive territory emerged from the

Introduction written by Annie BARTOLI, Martine BRASSEUR, Didier CHABAUD and Gilles ROUET.

work presented both as a project for society and as an approach to achieving it. At least three approaches could be distinguished: the establishment of a virtuous territorial dynamic (innovation, diversity, sustainable development, social equality), the fight against exclusion (unemployment, poverty, discrimination, dependence) and mobilization on a local project.

During the second workshop, the theme of the organization as an inclusive territory was explored in greater depth, in an attempt to provide answers to two main sets of questions. First of all, questions related to processes and dynamics were addressed: how are organizational inclusion practices built in a territory? What are the strategies of the different stakeholders in the projects or experiments? Is inclusion the goal or the means? Is it instrumentalized, or even hijacked, by the engineering of the systems implemented? The second series of questions addressed the apprehensions, forms and implications of inclusion. Indeed, many organizations, especially large businesses, have set up diversity departments and defined managerial strategies in favor of inclusion: what kind of inclusion is it? How do managers define it? What indicators can be used to monitor its evolution? Are the benefits of the actions carried out internally or within an area of activity concretely observable? What are the impacts on organizations' stakeholders?

The enlisting of organizations in the partnership dynamics established in a territory has, in particular, been identified as one of the conditions for success, whether these organizations designate private sector businesses or public or associative structures. Moreover, although the organization can be treated as one of the partners in a territory, it can also be analyzed as a space where the economic, social and societal dynamics that generate exclusion or inclusion interact, and then dynamics, being the bearers of inequalities and injustices, are factors of emancipation and diversity. Within local ecosystems, the weight of the managerial practices of large businesses carrying their own organizational culture is important, just as much as those of start-ups or those in force in historically established structures. They can influence or thwart the attempts of local actors carrying out an inclusive society project or, on the contrary, favor them or even stimulate them.

This movement and awareness seem to be growing in various places around the world. For example, at the end of August 2019, 34 multinationals pledged under the auspices of the Organization for Economic Cooperation and Development (OECD) to reduce all types of inequality and work towards inclusive growth as part of an alliance, the G7 Business for Inclusive Growth (B4IG). At the same time, leaders of the Business Round Table (BRT), a group of nearly 200 companies with combined revenues of $7 trillion, signed a manifesto on corporate purpose in which they pledged, among other things, to "support the communities in which they work".

Such advances might seem minimal, purely symbolic or even essentially an indicator of businesses' reluctance to make a true commitment to corporate social responsibility (CSR). Indeed, in 1981, the BRT had already published a declaration on corporate responsibility, which concluded that for each business "its entrepreneurial activities must have a social meaning just as its social activities must have an economic meaning", and in 1997 it reaffirmed, in a declaration on corporate governance, the essentiality of maximizing the profits of shareholders, thus marking a certain backward step that may have raised questions. Nevertheless, the more reaffirmed display of a desire to be a good corporate citizen confirms the evolution of mentalities and leads us to question the reality of practices and their effects. Moreover, all forms of organization appear to be concerned by the problem of developing territorial inclusion dynamics: they can take the form of residents' associations, public hospitals, units in the educational sector or even more informal structures.

Thus, inclusion can represent a project for the enterprise. This first book devoted to the theme of facilitating inclusion in a territory focuses more specifically on the role of organizations and entrepreneurial dynamics in inclusive approaches in territories. Two axes have been investigated: the first deals with the entrepreneurial dynamics identifiable in a territory (Part 1); the second delves into the social innovations of inclusive organizations (Part 2). The contributions include a study of the concept of inclusive territory in its general scope (Chapter 1) and analyses of inclusive social management practices in different countries (Chapters 2, 4, 5 and 6), as well as the exploration of specific strategies and tools, such as mobility processes in a logic of inclusion (Chapters 3 and 7) and diversity management approaches in local territories (Chapter 8).

In conclusion, the societal stakes of involving companies and organizations in the inclusive dynamics of a territory are highlighted and discussed. They are even more important in the context of a health crisis that has the indirect effect of aggravating inequalities and poverty. If inclusion, insofar as it is the bearer of a project for society, cannot be reduced to the fight against the various forms of exclusion and discrimination, the actions carried out very often emerge as the last resort for people in great distress.

PART 1

Entrepreneurial Dynamics that Promote Inclusion Within a Territory

1

Inclusive Territory:
An Ongoing Conceptualization

What does "inclusive territory" mean? The term is used increasingly often and seems to be used to guide research and management practices in order to solve a series of societal problems, the contours and nature of which are nonetheless vague and confusing. What territories are concerned? What kind of inclusion are we talking about? What is the aim behind choosing a formula combining both terms? Starting from the notion mobilized in the context of the specific practices of local partnerships, does the question raised lead to a conceptualization or even to the emergence of a theoretical current?

In this chapter, we highlight that, under the prism of inclusion, the territory is mainly defined as a space for the development of teleological ecosystems, whose *raison d'être* is social. An enterprise comes to play an essential role as an unavoidable partner and sometimes as an initiator of local dynamics. Its purpose is then questioned. Termed "inclusive", the territory thus symbolizes both a societal project and the collective mobilized to make it a reality.

To clarify what characterizes the inclusive approaches implemented in a territory, we rely on a review of the literature and on a thematic content analysis. Several angles of approach seem to be adopted, guiding different objects of study, from discrimination to the shortcomings of care networks and the lack of jobs. Beyond this variety, all researchers are united in

Chapter written by Martine BRASSEUR.

proposing models that reverse the traditional relationship between the economic and the social in order to achieve the same objective: the fight against exclusion.

Despite this, does the inclusive territory represent only an attempt to reverse the phenomena of exclusion? This would obscure an important dimension of the approaches involved, which is to take up the challenge of eradicating inequality and poverty. They can only achieve this by inventing new mechanisms and rethinking the notions of territory and inclusion. It is thus a question of stimulating a dynamic of social innovation while taking a different approach to the way we make society.

1.1. From economic territory to inclusive territory

As Pesqueux (2014, p. 60) points out, territory is a fuzzy concept. "It is about multiple references: geographical, historical, ethological, political, anthropological, economic and organizational." We might also add: sociological. The notion of inclusive territory does not escape the existence of multiple levels of analysis to define it. Many issues are also associated with it, preventing it from being positioned in a specific field and leading us to consider it as transdisciplinary. It finds its routes in the development of partnerships in a territory, which has given rise to numerous studies (Xhauf lair et al. 2010; Torre and Vollet 2015; de Beneditti et al. 2018; Hernandez 2018). Its legacy is therefore first and foremost that of understanding the territory from an economic perspective, as a business zone, a cluster, a competitiveness cluster to better position itself as a teleological ecosystem.

1.1.1. *A territory delimited historically by economics*

The activity area allows a spatial delimitation of the territory. It is not sufficient to specify the type of territory concerned insofar as its members may cohabit without any real collective dynamic. The term "cluster", in contrast, refers to networks of enterprises that are strongly anchored locally, often in the same niche or sector of production (Chalaye and Massard 2009; Torre and Zimmermann 2015). They can take the form of clusters of competitiveness, bringing very small enterprises and SMEs in the same field of activity together, with ad hoc associations of other actors depending on the context and initiatives. These clusters aim for pooling or collective action to increase their competitiveness. According to Retour (2008, p. 93), a competitiveness cluster is a "combination, in a given geographic area, of enterprises, training centers and public and private research units, which are committed to working together within the same structure, in order to generate synergies around common projects of an innovative nature with the critical mass necessary for international visibility". For the inclusive territory, we find the same mobilization of complementary actors around an innovative project. Despite this, although the competitiveness cluster is located in a territory, it does not define it, and both its stakes and positioning are international, making it vulnerable to the fluctuations of global markets (Suire and Vicente 2014). Moreover, the notion of competitiveness clearly orients its activity towards economic objectives.

It should be noted, however, that the social argument is not absent from local policies aimed at promoting clusters. Indeed, it is considered that clusters will lead to growth as a result of economic development and thus to an increase in employment and/or wages in growth markets. Several authors, such as Chatterji et al. (2014) for the United States, have undertaken to evaluate the systems put in place and have emphasized both the driving capacity for local development that clusters represent and the need to remain cautious about the effects observed. One of the major limitations of these forms of local partnership in networks of enterprises is that their impact on a territory remains selective (Fowler and Kleit 2014), which runs counter to an inclusive process. The populations targeted by employment are not indeed those who are the most disadvantaged because of a requirement in terms of skills. The dynamics imparted are not necessarily accompanied by a reduction in long-term unemployment, poverty or discrimination.

1.1.2. *A dynamic of coevolution with an inclusive goal*

The notion of an ecosystem seems to be closer to the dynamics at work or desired in an inclusive territory. Transposed by analogy to the business world by Moore (1993), it represents a metaphor drawn from the work of Tansley (1935), who is generally credited with being the first to define the concept to refer to the basic ecological unit made up of the environment and the organisms that live there. As Bateson (1972) pointed out, if the processes of coevolution are specific to any system, whether natural or social, and make it possible, by transposition, to characterize business, innovation and knowledge ecosystems, just like inclusive territories, two important differences are identifiable, both in relation to the first concept developed in ecology and between the types of ecosystem that have emerged in the field of enterprises.

The first major difference concerns the purpose of natural ecosystems. Without going into the philosophical debates that are still open, with reference in particular to Kant (2008, first published in 1790) and Spinoza (1993, originally published in 1677), the finality of nature, whether it exists or not, escapes both organisms and their natural environment: we cannot consider that natural ecosystems voluntarily self-orient their coevolution according to a project that they themselves have preconceived. In contrast, and without any generalization to all social ecosystems, when it comes to business, innovation, knowledge or, in this case, inclusion, the collective that the ecosystem represents (Moore 1996) sets itself objectives that constitute its *raison d'être*, without, however, as Kœnig (2012) points out, being able to really consider with Moore (1996, p. 61) that it "shares a community of destiny".

It would be more accurate to say, for the inclusive territory, that it makes the community's destiny its own. The impelled dynamics thus seem to move away from the mechanisms described by the founding theorists of the notion in ecology (Odum 1953), particularly for authors who assert the existence of a control pressure on the ecosystem (Moore 1993) exercised by one of the firms in the ecosystem (Pierce 2009) or by a dedicated body. On the contrary, they stand out as consistent with the principles of regulation defined in cybernetics (Wiener 1950) and more globally with the properties of totality, equifinality and homeostasis in systems (Bertalanffy 1966). It is in this sense that, in this chapter and in order to better understand what the notion of inclusive territory means, the ecosystems concerned will be described as teleological.

The second important difference is the one that seems to us to be able to both question the use of the term "ecosystem" in certain usages while affirming its relevance to the inclusive territory. Already emphasized by several authors (Fréry et al. 2012; Kœnig 2012), it concerns consideration of the environment within which the ecosystem actors are situated in a coevolution dynamic. Indeed, the reference to ecology implies taking the environment into account as one of the interacting parts in the constitution of an ecosystem. Yet, it seems to be forgotten in some definitions. Valkokari (2015) has therefore already examined the differences between the three types of ecosystems commonly distinguished in the world of enterprises to conclude that the rules of the game and the actors' representations are not the same in the business, innovation and knowledge ecosystems, whose orientations diverge while remaining generally centered on economic concerns and an international positioning. As far as business ecosystems are concerned, we can see that no term potentially referring to the environment in which they are located appears in the inventory of their components carried out by Moore (1996). Koenig (2012, p. 211) even went so far as to say that, for the notion of business ecosystems, if we do not reject the term, it was important "to define it without reference to ecology".

Nevertheless, some authors, such as Tolstykh et al. (2020), have shown that certain entrepreneurial ecosystems have an impact on the sustainable development of the region where they are anchored, although they consider this impact to be indirect. It is therefore not here again treated as consubstantial with the dynamics in progress, unlike the notion of inclusive territory, according to which the territory is the founder in an approach where it is a matter of boosting its coevolution in interrelation with the emergence of inclusive organizations and the commitment of the various partners following a process of joint transformations. From this angle, the notion of an inclusive territory is therefore closer to the concept of an ecosystem as it has been defined in ecology than the other ecosystems defined in the world of enterprises.

1.1.3. *A collaborative cross-sectoral partnership*

As with innovation or knowledge, inclusion requires mobilizing institutions or organizations from different activity areas. From public authorities to private businesses via charities or higher education and research establishments (Persais 2020), a local partnership is set up to respond to a shared problem. The nature of the project carried out by actors in the "inclusive territory" ecosystem is also a distinctive element that helps to characterize the shape of the partnership implemented. The initiatives taken to carry it out reverse the relationship between the economic and the social. Inclusion is no longer seen as a contingent positive consequence of economic development in a territory, assessed essentially in terms of job creation (Boutillier et al. 2016). It is the purpose and *raison d'être* of the ecosystem whose project is societal. The economy is only one means to achieve it in a collaborative social innovation process (Austin et al. 2006).

This collaborative approach is in line with current trends in the development of the socio-economic world, which "is not only made up of organizations, but also of collaborations between these organizations: [...] our economic reality is thus increasingly inter-organizational" (Defélix and Picq 2013, p. 42). In addition to intersectorality and its societal aim, however, there is a third specificity for the inclusive territory, inherent to both the territorial dynamics that are being promoted and the inclusion project. Thus, the concept of coopetition defined by Brandenburger and Nalebuff in 1996 allows us to grasp the modes of collaboration generally developed: a rational cooperation in a competitive universe. Moore (2006, p. 73) thus considered that business ecosystems "will require both cooperation and competition among their firms". For an inclusive goal, competition no longer makes sense either within ecosystems or between territories. As a result, unless we consider with Bengtsson and Kock (1999) that pure cooperation is a special case of coopetition without competition, it is uniquely cooperation that is at stake in inclusive territories and not coopetition. Moreover, several tensions commonly pointed out for any initiative with a societal vocation, such as those between the social and the economic or the individual and the collective, theoretically do not exist in the ecosystem of "inclusive territories". Unlike, for example, the social and solidarity economy (Audebrand 2017), the objective of the inclusive territory is not to propose a parallel economy but to solve societal problems.

1.2. From exclusion to inclusion

However, what does the inclusion project of "inclusive territory" ecosystems overlap with, and what inclusive approach do they implement? To further explore these notions, a thematic analysis of the content of the literature was conducted with two phases of article collection using keywords on the databases CAIRN, Science Direct and Business Source Premier. The two phases are presented in Table 1.1.

Two main findings emerged from the analysis. First, inclusion is addressed in response to a phenomenon of exclusion without it being specific to the territory concerned, even though it may be exacerbated there. Second, it characterizes the approach to problems identified by focusing on people in order to serve the general interest.

	First collection phase[1]	Second collection phase
Keywords	Inclusive territory Inclusive development	Territory + inclusion + exclusion *Cross-referencing of related concepts*: diversity/discrimination, CSR (corporate social responsibility), etc.
Number of items by theme	Territorial issues: 10 Problems of a social group: 9 Economic issues: 4 Other: 11	Territory: 35,184 items Inclusion: 1,551,389 items Exclusion: 833,774 items

Table 1.1. *The two collection phases of the thematic content analysis*

1.2.1. *A local response to a global exclusion problem*

In the articles reviewed, the development of an "inclusive territory" ecosystem was generally approached as a response to an exclusion problem. Concerning the forms of partnerships implemented, Seitanidi (2008) distinguishes three mobilization processes: reactive under external pressure, proactive in anticipation of a potential social risk and adaptive to counter an emerging problem. Overall, we have been able to identify two main orientations of approaches corresponding to a targeting: either a marginalized or discriminated population (women, the long-term unemployed, the dependent elderly, the disabled, etc.), or a disadvantaged territory (Seine-Saint-Denis in Île-de-France, certain African countries, some neighborhoods in New York, etc.).

---

1 The collected journals were: *Revue d'économie régionale et urbaine*; *Travail, genre et sociétés*; *Relations industrielles*; *Réalités industrielles*; *Management international*; *Vie sociale*; *European Journal of Disability Research*; *African Development Review*; *Nouvelle revue de l'adaptation et de la scolarisation*; *Annals of Public & Cooperative Economics*; *Annales françaises d'anesthésie et de réanimation*; *Géoéconomie*; *Retraite et société*; *Postcolonial Pragmatics*; *Journal of Pragmatics*; *Revue européenne de recherche sur le handicap*; *Mondes en développement*; *L'espace géographique*; and *Gérontologie et société*.

Concerning the focus on an excluded social group, we were able to find, in all the articles collected, the assertion that although this exclusion is an identifiable societal problem at the country level, and very often at the international level, it can only be dealt with at the regional level and by taking into account the particularities of the different contexts. The use of the term "inclusive territory" thus makes it possible to describe an approach aimed at eradicating a phenomenon of generalized exclusion by proceeding from the local to the global level. It poses the hypothesis that inclusion can only be achieved *through* the territory and no longer, following the many attempts often listed as ineffective, *on* the territories. We find the definition of the territory as an ecosystem encompassing both the local actors and their field of action: organisms and their environment.

In addition to the characterization of a pragmatic approach mobilizing good will "on the ground", the development of an inclusive territory has one of its foundations in the observation that the excluded population targeted by the system put in place is often trapped in a process of multiple forms of exclusion that are self-perpetuating. Discrimination keeps people out of work; unemployment leads to poverty, which limits or blocks access to information and knowledge, and also to healthcare, and reduces employment opportunities while stigmatizing the excluded. The authors draw on the work of economists and sociologists, such as Gazier (2010) and Banerjee and Duflo (2011), to support an argument that the reversal of this pernicious dynamic requires a global understanding of the local context of all these exclusions suffered by a given population.

Referring to the work of Paugam (1991), inclusion of the targeted social categories or groups cannot be met just with the establishment of help or support systems, which, although considered necessary for their survival in decent conditions, are also accused of keeping them in an inferior and devalued position. The inclusive territory approach is different. The objective is to develop a territory where the people concerned can escape from the social disqualification they have suffered. In contrast to traditional social practices, for example, in line with the work of Chevreuse (1979), the actions are no longer focused on an organization or an institution, but on a set of partner organizations and institutions. The question is no longer simply to find or preserve an inescapably precarious place for destitute individuals. It is to transform inclusion practices by considering the banishment of a given social category in a territory as a collective failure. Several works deal with care networks for the elderly, which are designed to preserve their lifestyles by keeping them at home in the city. Some have even coined a term for the inclusive territory thus constructed: the "gerontological territory" (Henrard 2010; Mahmoudi et al. 2010; Petitot et al. 2010; Vermorel and Rumeau 2010).

The focus on a disadvantaged territory seems to follow on from two observations: on the one hand, the existence of an "excluded territory" and, on the other hand, the intersectionality of exclusion phenomena. The first starts with a geographical territory that brings together populations in great poverty and creates a catalyst for all the markers of exclusion. Inequalities can then be identified no longer between social groups but between territories. Educational, health, digital and even generational fractures are then underlined between areas where the populations live. The notion of a territory is transformed by identification of the borders of a country, a region, a department, a city or even a neighborhood, grouping together the excluded just as much as they stigmatize them. These borders prove difficult to cross. Inclusive partnerships are therefore developed for an entire territory. They are mobilized with actions that aim to promote a social mix and diversity, others that aim to generate bridges giving access to training, employment and culture and still others that aim to identify and make visible the territory's resources in order to change its image.

Following the philosopher Corine Pelluchon (2011), it is the view of a vulnerable and/or different Other, a discriminated social group or an excluded territory, that is questioned. In this approach, the inclusive territory presents several important characteristics that can be found in research before the notion of the inclusive territory became popular and in studies that aim to question the notion of territory:

– construction of a space for action by the actors (Friedmann and Weaver 1979; Raffestin 1980);

– "active" understanding of the territory (Pesqueux 2014);

– the proximity and collaboration of actors as a territorial resource (Colletis and Pecqueur 1993; Rodet-Kroichvili 2018);

– the possibility of informality as a condition for success (Njifen 2014);

– "open" locations in the sense of a dynamic territory allowing for recomposition and overlap (Barabel et al. 2009; Torre 2018).

1.2.2. *Serving people in the general interest*

The second phase of data collection explored the notion of inclusion in greater depth. It is often linked to the concept of diversity and the rebirth of singularities, thus time as resources (Shore et al. 2011; Nishii 2013). It is therefore distinguished from integration, which, on the one hand, approaches differences as constraints or shortcomings (Plaisance et al. 2007) and, on the other hand, corresponds to a requirement of social conformity to norms or a dominant culture (Pitsis et al. 2004). In contrast, inclusion in organizations is associated with the development of a sense of belonging to the same work community in a civic conception of collective life that respects the well-being and autonomy of individuals (Bouquet 2015).

Inclusive practices thus seem to be constructed according to what Morin (1990a) would call a dialogical principle, i.e. according to two opposing and indissociable logics that are linked into a unity in the maintenance of their duality: the development of the cohesion of a collective and the affirmation of the individualities of its members. From this perspective, inclusion can be understood as the attempt to permanently reconcile two forces, one centripetal, generating similarities and proceeding by assimilating individuals into a community, the other centrifugal and "atomizing", maintaining heterogeneity and social distance. The possibility of inclusion could be seen as illusory, which some authors, such as Gillig (2006) for the inclusion of disabled students in school, have questioned.

Generally speaking, partnerships between organizations are implemented with the "imperative to realize benefits for the wider community rather than for special interests" (Sullivan and Skelcher 2002, p. 752). Although the purpose of the inclusive territory is clearly part of this quest, the notion of general interest that is its object is nonetheless undefinable (Rangeon 1986). The use of the expression, which is very widespread in the political domain of public administration or within certain enterprises, can lead to it being diverted from its original meaning of "everyone's interest", deriving the interest of the State or of an institution (Lascoumes and Le Bourhis 1998). Concerning the inclusive territory, the concern for the general interest asserted at the level of a territory transcends not only personal but organizational interests: within the ecosystem, each party acts in concert for the whole. Several studies have questioned the managerial repercussions induced by these approaches generally re-situated in a stance of corporate social responsibility (CSR), as outlined recently in a collective work by Rey and Vivès (2020). The authors confirm the impetus of a coevolution dynamic for the composites of the inclusive territory in interrelation with the environment.

Moreover, the intersectoriality of organizational partnerships is accompanied by the necessary individual commitment of the target population and the consideration of territorial particularities and dynamics. Several studies have shown that the motivations of partners to engage in teleological ecosystems are multiple. In the same way, the impact of the systems implemented can be apprehended in different ways (van Tulder et al. 2016), opening a debate on the evaluation methods to be implemented and on the interpretation in terms of success or failure of the approaches sometimes initiated with public aid. For inclusive territories, a critical stance can be adopted concerning indicators of success and an approach of assessment by results. Is not inclusion observable from the very first initiative of an inclusive territory because of its integration of previously excluded populations into the system?

Any action implemented is thus inherently inclusive. This implies, of course, that these populations, the targets of inclusion, are not treated as objects of the ecosystem project implemented, but as one of its components. The contrary would be paradoxical, unless the reification of the excluded and the impossibility of evaluating the systems represent the limits or potential abuses of the systems implemented.

In any case, inclusion operates in a relationship between the individual and the collective, which we describe as dialogical in reference to Morin (1990b), i.e. in an association of two different logics that can be considered both antagonistic and complementary, one affirming the singularity of individuals and the second seeking their assimilation, while maintaining this duality in the unity sought. The notion of inclusion used by actors in inclusive territories can thus be enlightened by the concept of reliance (Morin 2004, p. 239), while positioning the problem to be solved in the field of ethics: reliance is "activating", while "linking" is participating and "linked" passive. Inclusion thus seems to emerge as an act of reliance "with an other, reliance with a community, with a society and, at the limit, reliance with the human species", which, for Morin (2004, p. 16), defines the moral act.

1.3. Conclusion

The inclusive territory is thus a notion in the process of being questioned theoretically and which, as a result, after having designated observable practices in a solely pragmatic apprehension, is in the process of becoming a concept, according to the distinction clarified by Dumez (2011). Indeed, we have emphasized the existence of a dynamic interaction between its naming, understanding and extension, which is consistent with Ogden and Richards' (1923) method of defining concepts.

The studies already carried out, and to which this book bears witness, may even suggest opening a field of research taking itself as its object. It would still be in the phase of clearing and identifying the lines of investigation to be developed. One of them seems to us to relate to the question of temporality in the inclusive territorial dynamics impelled within the ecosystems mobilized: are inclusive territories ephemeral or can permanence be envisaged? Sewell's distinction (2005) between the teleological, the experimental and the event-driven or the work of Bouba-Olga and Grossetti (2018) on the stabilization of virtuous dynamics could undoubtedly represent relevant analytical supports to provide elements of response, or even to define typologies between the different systems implemented. Are inclusive territories actually inclusive? And if they are, to what extent do they remain so?

1.4. References

Audebrand, L.K. (2017). Expanding the scope of paradox scholarship on social enterprise: The case for (re)introducing worker cooperatives. *M@n@gement*, 20(4), 368–393.

Austin, J.E., Stevenson, H., Wei-Skillem, J. (2006). Social and commercial entrepreneurship: The same, different or both? *Entrepreneurship Theory and Practice*, 30(1), 1–22.

Banerjee, A.V. and Duflo, E. (2011). *Poor Economics. A Radical Rethinking of the Way to Fight Global Poverty*. Public Affairs, New York.

Barabel, M., Chabault, D., Meier, O., Tixier, J. (2009). La dynamique de territoire et l'évolution d'un pôle de compétitivité : le cas de Cosmetic Valley. *Management et Avenir*, 25, 144–163.

Bateson, G. (1972). *Steps to an Ecology of Mind*. Ballantine Books, New York.

de Beneditti, J., Geindre, S., Dominguez-Pery, C. (2018). Les écosystèmes des pôles de compétitivité. Dynamique et choix de modèle d'affaires. *Revue française de gestion*, 272, 139–154.

Bengtsson, M. and Kock, S. (1999). Cooperation and competition in relationships between competitors in business networks. *Journal of Business and Industrial Marketing*, 14(3), 178–194.

Bertalanffy, L.V. (1966). Histoire et méthode de la théorie générale des systèmes. *Atomes*, 21, 100–104.

Bouba-Olga, O. and Grossetti, M. (2018). La mythologie CAME (Compétitivité, Attractivité, Métropolisation, Excellence) : comment s'en désintoxiquer ? *HAL* [Online]. Available at: https://hal.archives-ouvertes.fr/hal-01724699v2.

Bouquet, B. (2015). L'inclusion : approche socio-sémantique. *Vie sociale*, 11, 15–25.

Boutillier, S., Levratto, N., Carre, D. (2016). *Entrepreneurial Ecosystems*. ISTE Ltd, London, and John Wiley & Sons, New York.

Brandenburger, A. and Nalebuff, B.J. (1996). *Co-Opetition*. Currency Doubleday, New York.

Chalaye, S. and Massard, N. (2009). Clusters: Diverse practices and performance measurement. *Revue d'économie industrielle*, 128(4), 153–176.

Chatterji, A., Glaeser, E., Kerr, W. (2014). Clusters of entrepreneurship and innovation. *Innovation Policy and the Economy*, 14(1), 129–166.

Chevreuse, C. (1979). *Pratiques inventives du travail social*. Les Éditions Ouvrières, Paris.

Clarysse, B., Wright, M., Bruneel, J., Mahajan, A. (2014). Creating value in ecosystems: Crossing the chasm between knowledge and business ecosystems. *Research Policy*, 43(7), 1164–1176.

Colletis, G. and Pecqueur, B. (1993). Intégration des espaces et quasi-intégration des firmes : vers de nouvelles rencontres productives ? *Revue d'économie régionale et urbaine*, 3, 489–508.

Defélix, C. and Picq, T. (2013). De l'entreprise étendue à la "gestion des compétences étendues" : enjeux et pratiques en pôles de compétitivité. *@GRH*, 7, 41–66.

Dumez, H. (2011). Qu'est-ce qu'un concept ? *Le Libellio d'Aegis*, 7(1), 65–79.

Fowler, C.S. and Kleit, R.G. (2014). The effects of industrial clusters on the poverty rate. *Economic Geography*, 90(2), 129–154.

Fréry, F., Gratacap, A., Isckia, T. (2012). Les écosystèmes d'affaires, par-delà la métaphore. *Revue française de gestion*, 222, 69–75.

Friedmann, J. and Weaver, C. (1979). *Territory and Function. The Evolution of Regional Planning*. University of California Press, Berkeley.

Gazier, B. (2010). La discrimination économique est-elle soluble dans la complexité ? *Revue de l'OFCE*, 114, 45–64.

Gillig, J.M. (2006). L'illusion inclusive ou le paradigme artificiel. *La nouvelle revue de l'adaptation et de la scolarisation*, 36, 119–126.

Henrard, J.C. (2010). Territoires gérontologiques : la question en France au regard d'autres pays européens. *Gérontologie et Société*, 33(1), 123–128.

Hernandez, S. (2018). Management territorial paradoxal : le cas des espaces agricoles périurbains. *Revue internationale des sciences administratives*, 84, 557–575.

Kant, I. (2008). *Critique of Judgement*. Oxford University Press.

Koenig, G. (2012). Note de recherche : le concept d'écosystème d'affaires revisité. *M@n@gement*, 15(2), 208–224.

Lascoumes, P. and Le Bourhis, J.P. (1998). Le bien commun comme construit territorial. Identités d'action et procédures. *Politix*, 11(42), 37–66.

Mahmoudi, R., Vanhaecke, C., Jolly, D., Blanchard, F., Dramé, M., Novella, J.L. (2010). Quelques réflexions sur les "vieux" et les territoires gérontologiques. *Gérontologie et Société*, 33(1), 87–93.

Moore, J.F. (1993). Predators and prey: A new ecology of competition. *Harvard Business Review*, 71(3), 75–86.

Moore, J.F. (1996). *The Death of Competition: Leadership and Strategy in the Age of Business Ecosystems*. Harper Collins, New York.

Moore, J.F. (2006). Business ecosystems and the view from the firm. *The Antitrust Bulletin*, 51(1), 31–75.

Morin, E. (1990a). *Science avec conscience*. Le Seuil, Paris.

Morin, E. (1990b). *Introduction à la pensée complexe*. ESF, Paris.

Morin, E. (2004). *La méthode. Éthique*. Le Seuil, Paris.

Nishii, L.H. (2013). The benefits of climate for inclusion for gender-diverse groups. *Academy of Management Journal*, 56(6), 1754–1774.

Njifen, I. (2014). L'informalité : un nouveau paradigme de développement et d'intégration "par le bas" en Afrique. *African Development Review*, 26, 21–32.

Odum, E.P. (1953). *Fundamentals of Ecology*. Saunders, Philadelphia.

Ogden, C. and Richards, I. (1923). *The Meaning of Meaning. A Study of the Influence of Language Upon Thought and of the Science of Symbolism*. Brace and World, New York.

Paugam, S. (1991). *La disqualification sociale*. PUF, Paris.

Pelluchon, C. (2011). *Éléments pour une éthique de la vulnérabilité. Les hommes, les animaux, la nature*. Éditions du Cerf, Paris.

Persais, E. (2020). Vers une approche inclusive des écosystèmes entrepreneuriaux. Le cas de French AssurTech. *Revue française de gestion*, 286, 107–132.

Pesqueux, Y. (2014). De la notion de territoire. *Prospective et Stratégie*, 4(5), 55–68.

Petitot, C., Beard, J., Kalache, A., Plouffe, L., Cox, J., Powell, S., Tahrat, A.M. (2010). Vers des environnements-amis des aînés. *Gérontologie et Société*, 33(1), 229–242.

Pierce, L. (2009). Big losses in ecosystem niches: How core firm decisions drive complementary product shakeouts. *Strategic Management Journal*, 30(3), 323–247.

Pitsis, T.S., Kornberger, M., Clegg, S.R. (2004). The art of managing relationships in interorganizational collaboration. *M@n@gement*, 7(3), 47–67.

Plaisance, E., Belmont, B., Vérillon, A., Schneider, C. (2007). Intégration ou inclusion ? Éléments pour contribuer au débat. *La nouvelle revue de l'adaptation et de la scolarisation*, 3, 159–164.

Raffestin, C. (1980). *Pour une géographie du pouvoir*. LITEC, Paris.

Rangeon, F. (1986). *L'idéologie de l'intérêt général*. Economica, Paris.

Retour, D. (2008). Pôles de compétitivité, propos d'étape. *Revue française de gestion*, 190, 93–99.

Rey, F. and Vivès, C. (eds) (2020). *Le monde des collectifs. Enquête sur les recompositions du travail*. Éditions Teseo, Paris.

Rodet-Kroichvili, N. (2018). Proximités des acteurs de la relation d'emploi et arrangements locaux d'emploi et de travail en France. *Revue d'économie régionale urbaine*, 5, 1313–1348.

Seitanidi, M.M. (2008). Adaptative responsibilities: Non-linear interactions across social sectors. Cases from cross sector social partnerships. *Emergence*, 10(3), 51–64.

Sewell, W.H. (2005). *Logics of History. Social Theory and Social Transformation*. University of Chicago Press.

Shore, L.M., Randel, A.E., Chung, B.G., Dean, M.A., Erhart, K.H., Singh, G. (2011). Inclusion and diversity in work groups: A review and model for future research. *Journal of Management*, 37(4), 1262–1289.

Spinoza, B. (1993). L'Éthique. Démontrée selon la méthode géométrique et divisée en cinq parties [Online]. Available at: http://classiques.uqac.ca/classiques/spinoza/ethique/ethique_de_Spinoza.pdf.

Suire, R. and Vicente, J. (2014). Clusters for life or life cycles of clusters: In search of the critical factors of clusters' resilience. *Entrepreneurship and Regional Development*, 26(1/2), 142–164.

Sullivan, H. and Skelcher, C. (2002). *Working Across Boundaries. Collaboration in Public Services*. Palgrave Macmillan, New York.

Tansley, A.G. (1935). The use and abuse of vegetational concepts and terms. *Ecology*, 16(3), 284–307.

Tolstykh, T., Gamidullaeva, L., Shmeleva, N., Wozniak, M., Vasin, S. (2020). An assessment of regional sustainability via the maturity level of entrepreneurial ecosystems. *Journal of Open Innovation*, 7(5) [Online]. Available at: https://doi.org/10.3390/joitmc7010005.

Torre, A. (2018). Les moteurs du développement territorial. *Revue d'économie régionale urbaine*, 4, 711–736.

Torre, A. and Vollet, D. (eds) (2015). *Partenariats pour le développement territorial*. Éditions Quæ, Versailles.

Torre, A. and Zimmermann, J.B. (2015). From clusters to local industrial ecosystems. *Revue d'économie industrielle*, 152(4), 13–38.

Valkokari, K. (2015). Business, innovation, and knowledge ecosystems: How they differ and how to survive and thrive within them. *Technology Innovation Management Review*, 5(8), 17–24.

Van Tulder, R., Seitanidi, M., Crane, A., Brammer, S. (2016). Enhancing the impact of cross-sector partnerships. Four impact loops for channeling partnership studies. *Journal of Business Ethics*, 135, 1–17.

Vermorel, M. and Rumeau, E. (2010). Les inter-filières sanitaires et médico-sociales gérontologiques : une approche fonctionnelle de la notion de territoire. *Gérontologie et Société*, 33(1), 213–221.

Wiener, N. (1950). *The Human Use of Human Beings: Cybernetics and Society*. Houghton Mifflin Company, Boston.

Xhauflair, V., Pichault, F., Maesschalck, M.F. (2010). Partenariats inter-organisationnels et nouvelles formes de gouvernance : les conditions d'un compromis équilibré et pérenne. *Management et Avenir*, 33, 298–316.

2

The Employer Group and its Stakeholders: Application for a Timeshare HR Manager Job

At a time when networking SMEs and VSEs has become an essential strategy for competitiveness (Smith et al. 1995; Habhab-Rave 2009), where the success of a company is strongly linked to the success of its network (Lambert and Cooper 2000), the territory seems to offer new opportunities for the development of companies and in particular for the HR function (Colin and Mercier 2017). The favoring of such networking between geographically close companies, employer groups (EGs from now on), arises from a specific legal form making it possible to establish a network of SMEs. It can play a role that remains, however, "largely underestimated" (Lethielleux and André 2018, p. 222).

Based on a principle of pooling skills between companies in the same territory that could not afford these skills alone, the EGs, whether they take the form of associations or cooperatives, make it possible to meet both business flexibility needs (mainly VSEs and SMEs) and employee security needs. The latter have only one employer, the EG, with timesharing missions distributed between several entities with the aim of achieving full-time employment through networking. With the essential mission of maintaining jobs locally, the EGs present themselves as a lever for the development, revitalization and attractiveness of territories.

Chapter written by Anne JOYEAU, Sébastien LE GALL and Gwénaëlle POILPOT-ROCABOY.

The stakes are therefore also societal, going beyond the bounds of the company. In its highly regulated French legal form, the group of employers has specific French characteristics, with alternatives that exist abroad, in Canada, for example, in the form of cooperative modes.

Paradoxically, despite an institutionalization recognized legally for more than 30 years and despite a French economic fabric marked by the strong presence of VSEs and SMEs, EGs remain, even today, in a kind of "invisibility" (Lethielleux 2018, p. 212). Faced with this paradox, we propose to analyze the EG mechanism and, more specifically, the conditions for success in the network it forms with its stakeholders (employees made available, companies). Our objective is to understand the mechanisms that explain the success, often local, of this form of employment timesharing (CESE 2018).

2.1. The employer group and its stakeholders: A network at the service of a territorialized HRM

After showing how the timeshare employment network built around the EG meets the definition of inter-organizational networks, an analysis of the literature allows us to identify the conditions for success associated with such networks (section 2.1.1). We then specify the stakes of the timeshare network, in particular for HRM and for the timeshare HR manager profession. The virtuous effects of the deployment of this profession within SMEs are identified at three levels: individual, organizational and territorial (section 2.1.2).

2.1.1. The conditions for a successful inter-organizational network

Described as early as the 1980s as an intermediate form between market and hierarchy by Thorelli (1986), the network can be defined as "a group of nodes more or less connected by a set of links" (Mandard 2015, p. 4). The unique nature of any network lies in the interconnection (Torre 2016), as well as the pursuit of common needs (Boulanger 1990). From a dyad to an infinite number of connections, the network can therefore be any size. Inter-organizational networks can be formal with contractual links or, conversely, informal. Today the expression of a particular form of organization, the network particularly concerns small firms, "which will take advantage of their flexible organization to pool their resources and thus benefit from the famous positive network externalities" (Torre 2016, p. 462). Among the key dimensions related to the analysis of networks, the spatial dimension is, for some authors, almost a given (Torre 2016). Due to the importance of relationships taking place within a determined geographical perimeter, and between local actors, we can see the emergence of territorialized networks. For some, like Carluer (2006, p. 209), "local rootedness [...] is now sought in the perspective of a reticular connection, favorable to externalities of all kinds (pecuniary, technological, but above all relational and informational)".

EGs appeared in France with the law of January 25, 1985, in order to allow SMEs in the same territory to group together and employ a workforce that they could not afford to recruit alone. The EG is thus the result of a specific inter-organizational configuration within the framework of a formal network that, by definition, "structures social or economic relations between entities based on a proven and recognized institutional dimension" (Torre 2016, p. 458). The pooling of human resources allows member firms to have access to skills that each of them, taken individually, could not employ full time for reasons of cost, the seasonality of their activities or workload.

This tripartite employment relationship – companies in the same territory, employees, EGs – makes it possible to reconcile contradictory requirements linked to the impact of the evolution of the environment (economic, technological, social, etc.) on the company's need for flexibility and the employee's need for relative stability and security. Thus, the EG makes it possible to transform occasional or timeshare needs into full-time open-ended contracts by pooling employment management. The member companies in the grouping may come from the same sector (agricultural EGs, single-sector EGs) or from several private commercial sectors (multi-sector EGs) or associations (EGs for not-for-profit associations) and share the same need for timeshare skills or the same objective (EGs for integration and qualification). The timeshare employee has a single employment contract (single contract and salary): their employer is the EG (single employer) and they are made available to two or more member companies of the EG. The EG is part of the innovative managerial practices of employment and skills management that place locally rooted inter-organizational partnerships at the heart of the crucial issues of the flexibility and adaptability of organizations. According to Xhauflair et al. (2010, p. 314), these are "new social compromises" in terms of social regulation.

The central element in the definition of a network appears to be cooperation between actors (Mandard 2015). However, as soon as this "network configuration" leads to a confrontation between the network's logics of competitiveness, on the one hand, and those of the different firms, on the other hand, the question of the network's durability arises (Géniaux and Mira-Bonnardel 2003). Thus, the criterion of the network's success seems to be naturally (mechanically) induced: it is necessary, in order to ensure the network's sustainability, that the commitment of the network's stakeholders is sustainable (Loufrani-Fedida and Saint-Germes 2018). It is a matter of bringing about, among the network's stakeholders, a balanced and sustainable compromise (Xhauflair et al. 2010).

Analysis of the network's conditions for success therefore requires a clear identification of the profiles of the various stakeholders and their interest in participating. It also seems necessary to verify that the balance of power between the actors is not asymmetrical, at the risk of leading to situations that are "unbalanced and untenable in the long term, because they are too insecure for the actors concerned" (Xhauflair et al. 2010, p. 299). In the case of the timeshare network, three types of actors are involved: the EG – as an associative or cooperative structure – the member companies and the employees made available. As Xhauflair et al. (2010, p. 312) point out, "in contexts that are unstable and full of uncertainty, the implementation of a new form of governance is not natural". Indeed, there is always a risk that it will appear beneficial to one of the parties, to the detriment of the others, at least in the short term. This is also the warning issued by Albert Cromarias (2012), who highlights the indispensable nature of the search for compromise in the case of sports EGs, a compromise that must be activated by one (or more) identified individual(s) or project leader(s) within the network. If, by definition, a network is made up of several autonomous partners, they are mutually dependent on each other to achieve common objectives (Boulanger 1990), with governance mechanisms based on relationships of trust and partnership (Ettigghoffer and Van Beneden 2000), the circulation of information and the complementarity of skills (Assens and Courie-Lemeur 2014). The notion of common goals, of a common task (Smith et al. 1995), made explicit in a transparent way, seems essential. The absence of clear objectives and definitions of roles appears to be a source of ambiguity. The issue of meaning-making becomes central for stakeholders (Chedotel and Viviani 2016). In particular, Loufrani-Fedida and Saint-Germes (2018) note that, in the context of a territorial project, the commitment dynamic is strongly anchored in the territory, which would play a unifying role for the actors. Is there a common goal of the EG and its stakeholders? What is it? Is there convergence on the meaning given to the network?

As Chedotel and Viviani (2016) report from a broad analysis of the literature, the dynamics of sustainable cooperation in networks seem to come up against various obstacles: trust, the basis of a successful cooperation (Torre 2016), which can evolve positively or negatively over time or depend on the nature of the territory, and the diversity of professional identities (Chedotel 2004). This last question arises in particular in the case of the EG. Indeed, compared to other forms of inter-organizational networks in the field of employment, such as temporary work, EGs, according to Lethielleux (2018), modify the wage relationship on several levels, two of which are noteworthy because they are very specific to this network: that of hierarchical power (a de jure employer differs from the de facto employer) and, by induction, that of the identities at work.

Through these two aspects, EGs disrupt the norms and organization of work (Lethielleux 2018). In this context, questions related to the employee's sense of belonging (to the de jure employer and/or to the de facto employer) arise. Finally, in the context of a local network such as the one built by the EG, the territory becomes a key player in the system, "a stakeholder in its own right, a player in the governance" (Colin and Mercier 2017, p. 110), which must therefore be added to the timeshare network. Although the question of territory is an old question in HRM in the case of paternalistic companies, it is still central today in the case of the company-network affirming its social and societal responsibility (Hommel 2006). In terms of employment and skills management and skills, the characteristics of the territory are therefore decisive.

At the end of this overview of inter-organizational networks and of what are posed as the conditions of a network's success (this being defined as its durability and sustainability through a balanced compromise and by meeting the satisfaction of each group of actors), different factors must be taken into account to judge the success of the timeshare network led by the EG:

– the interests of the various stakeholders, whether the network is meeting their needs and the symmetry of the relationships within the network;

– convergence on the meaning given to the timeshare network;

– the potential obstacles to be removed and levers, such as employees' feeling of belonging;

– the characteristics of the territory favorable to the timeshare network.

In order to serialize our analysis, we choose to focus not on a particular type of EG, but on a specific profession, that of the timeshare HR manager. The societal issues surrounding this profession, at a time when the figure of the HRM is seen as a "network man" (Colin and Mercier 2017, p. 119), seem to us to be crucial and, simultaneously, the existence of this profession within EGs seems rare, despite the widespread beneficial effects when the timeshare network is functioning.

2.1.2. The virtuous effects of the timeshare network through the example of an HR manager

The EG seems to be the source of a "win-win" relationship for companies, territories and employees (Lethielleux 2018, p. 4). Analysis of existing jobs shows that all professions can be exercised in a timesharing framework. The job of "HR manager" seems to us to be particularly important for the development of companies and their territory, with strong stakes in terms of competitiveness for SMEs and the permanent and crucial challenges of productivity and flexibility. Due to the way they work, EGs can provide a relevant response to SMEs, for which the HR role is not always perceived as a priority, despite difficulties in recruiting, a lack of candidate motivation and the legal and administrative complexity imposed by the Labor Code (Vilette 2008; Lethielleux and André 2018). Paradoxically, in such a context, the job of timeshare HR manager still remains underdeveloped in companies (Joyeau and Poilpot-Rocaboy 2014).

Some studies have already looked at the virtuous effects of the timeshare HR manager. Two types of effects have been identified: on the timeshare employee and on the SME manager. For the employee, integrating a timeshare HR manager in an SME has a number of advantages (Joyeau and Poilpot-Rocaboy 2014; Joyeau et al. 2016):

– a diversity of tasks that induces a rapid and dense acquisition of skills and thus an increase in employability, which is a response to the demand for escape from certain employees, to the absence of routines;

– a richness of exchanges, creating social links due to an intensity of communication for the timeshare HR manager. It is essential teamwork and multi-site work that establish its territorial recognition;

– financial security and job stability with the avoidance of precarious or short-term contracts and less anxiety in cases of termination of the contract in one of the companies.

For the manager, the recruitment of a shared HR manager in an SME via an EG is not without an impact on their health. In a context where the dual role of MD and HR manager seems difficult to bear (Joyeau et al. 2018b), the use of a shared HR manager offers a whole range of resources. Thus, the presence of the HR manager provides employees with newly freed-up time, the establishment of an emotional and relational delegation and the acquisition of HR expertise. These resources produce both direct effects for the SME manager (by reducing stress and regaining a sense of purpose in their job as manager) and indirect effects (thanks to more efficient HR management leading to better company performance). In return, these positive effects on their health are themselves new resources, enabling them to enter a "success spiral", in the sense of Hobfoll (1989).

On the business side, the advantages of hiring a timeshare HR manager are primarily related to the development of "flexicurity" (Joyeau and Poilpot-Rocaboy 2014): flexibility for the company and simultaneously security for employees. Flexicurity is a means of attracting employees who are looking for a stable job, despite a limited need in the company, and a response to a short-term need, including rare or expensive skills, in a permanent manner. Another considerable advantage identified lies in the creation of value through access to external skills in a network, which only the timeshare formula allows, by providing the following:

– access to HR expertise that has significant perspective due to non-daily presence in the company;

– a source of innovation because of the various experiences and the outside view of the timesharing HR manager;

– an opportunity to develop a professional network for SMEs.

Finally, as mentioned above, because it frees the SME manager from their HR mission and because it allows them to refocus on their core business of strategic management of their company, the use of a timesharing HR manager becomes a real lever for developing the company (Joyeau et al. 2017). Going beyond the boundaries of the company via a network logic, timesharing also presents itself as a solution for dealing with staff and skills shortages on a territorial scale (Joyeau and Poilpot-Rocaboy 2016; Lethielleux 2018). Contributions can be direct, with greater attractiveness due to specific skills maintained in the territory thanks to strengthened HRM practices in companies, sharing and transfer of good practices and, therefore, inter-company synergy effects. They can occur more indirectly, with interconnected effects between the development of the company and that of the territory.

Thus, the job of timeshare HR manager via an EG, when the network is functioning, presents considerable virtues at three levels: from an individual point of view, with positive effects on the timeshare HR manager employees and on the health of the SME manager; at the organizational level, with effects on the social and economic performance of the company; finally, at the territorial level, on the performance of local companies and on the employment and attractiveness of the territory. The added value of the presence of a timeshare HR manager is therefore certain, shared between the companies, the timeshare HR manager employees and the territory. The challenge of defining the conditions that enable EGs to manage their relations with their stakeholders in the best possible way within the framework of the deployment of the HR function thus appears essential.

2.2. The employer group and its stakeholders: Cross-references on the conditions for success

To identify the conditions for success, we opted for a qualitative methodology, with a series of 11 interviews (Table 2.12) conducted in early 2019. The research was intended to be exploratory. The objective was to cross-reference the view points of the network's various stakeholders (EG, SME manager, employees made available) on their perception of the conditions for success. Thus, on the EG side, we met with six managers:

three directors and three local managers whose primary mission was to manage relations with stakeholders (employees, companies) in specific territories (most often on the scale of an employment basin). On the business side, two SME managers (members and directors) were interviewed.

Finally, we also collected the perceptions of three time-sharing HR managers within EGs (Table 2.12). Each interview lasted between one and two hours, using a semi-directive technique following an interview grid based on three themes presented in Table 2.13. For each interview, the objective was to identify the conditions for the effects identified as virtuous to occur, while ensuring that these virtuous effects were in the interest of all parties. In other words, how to qualify the success of the deployment of a timeshare HR manager via an EG? In terms of the network's conditions for success, it was also a question of understanding the specificities of those of the EG relative to those identified from a theoretical point of view. Each interview was re-transcribed and the content analysis was carried out manually, using a mixed coding – both emergent and pre-established according to the questions arising from the literature review.

The results are presented in three stages. After having confirmed the representations of the success criterion according to the network's stakeholders (section 2.2.1), we question the profiles of each member of the network that appear to be adapted (section 2.2.2) and then the nature and quality of the required relationships (section 2.2.3).

2.2.1. *The diversity of representations of the success criterion*

The diversity of representations of the success criterion emerges (Table 2.1). For the EGs, the success criterion is the capacity of the HR manager to profoundly and sustainably transform the company's HR practices. It also depends on the quality of the support provided to the timeshare employees. For SME managers, success results from adapting the time and skills made available to meet the needs expressed. For timeshare HR managers, success is the result of the company's growth, which leads to the enrichment of these missions.

MD-EG1	"When the training plan doubled or tripled. When employee turnover disappeared. When the accident rate decreased. We realized that to achieve this result, it wasn't just a matter of time, but also a matter of shared skills."
EGM2	"The goal is really to support employees in their career path. That's what we're all about."
SME1	"The company, when there are 20 of us, we rely on timesharing. This makes it possible to anchor the skill in the company. It can't afford to take on a full-time person."
HRM1	"That the company grows and the position grows as a result."

Table 2.1. *The diversity of representations of the success criterion*

For EGs, the success of timesharing also depends on a quantitative assessment, whether this is based on the number of jobs created or on the economic performance of the association (Table 2.2).

MD-EG1	"We only live from our turnover and from the sale of our services. And if our services aren't growing in volume, it's because we have a problem, it's because we don't look as good as we could. It's that our work is not as recognized."
MD-EG2	"For me, a success is when there are more than 10 or 15 people in the same profession in a small area like mine, with 300,000 inhabitants. There, we can say that there is a real territorial need."
MD-EG3	"As the director of labor says: 'How many SMEs are there on the territory that have created so many jobs in 19 years?' That's not wrong. But at the same time, I say to myself that timesharing remains confidential."
EGM1	"Like any business, we have a duty to maintain an economic turnover."

Table 2.2. *Quantitative assessment of success*

However, network actors find it difficult to identify explicit success criteria for timesharing for HR (Table 2.3).

EGM2	"There's a kind of magic that happens. Why? Because you put care into it, I think. We put a lot of energy into it."
EGM1	"It's an almost magical balance. We're in a good position to know that for the same employee at different companies, you can get different returns."
EGM2	"I have great stories of leaders who were not convinced, and then after a while realize what it brings."
EGM2	"It's lace, it's fine work."
EGM3	"We call it 'high fashion.' What we call 'mesh' changes on a very regular basis."

Table 2.3. *Difficult-to-identify success criteria*

The expressions used by managers in connection with the stakeholders involved in the EGs reflect this perception: "a magic that happens", "beautiful stories". These managers also testify to the meticulousness that this implies for each provision: "lace", "high fashion".

A significant divergence emerged on one criterion for successful deployment of a timesharing HR manager. This divergence appears both at the level of the different actors of the network and also sometimes within the same EG according to the function occupied. It refers to the evolution of the position of timeshare HR manager who, very regularly after a few years, performs this function on a full-time basis within one of the member companies (Table 2.4). This integration can be considered virtuous insofar as it reflects the recognition of this function initially created through timesharing. Nevertheless, the EG then loses a timeshare employee and a company in the network, which leads to the weakening of its economic model.

This scenario reflects the EG's regular difficulty in asserting the added value of maintaining a shared HR position over time to its member companies.

MD-EG1	"We have a success rate for recruitment that is monstrous, as perceived by the members. You hire someone, they go to work, they're happy. Everything is fine. Except that they steal them from us. My success is that after four years, he's still here."
EGM3	"We have a high turnover, which we call positive, where our timeshare employees move on to full time. This is part of our business. It's also a guarantee of professionalism, of good recruitment. It's not a big deal. It is also the recognition of the grouping on its employment basin. But in HR jobs, it's often very quick."
HRM3	"And then there are also some rather positive situations in timesharing. I knew an HR person who arrived after me, who was hired on a timeshare basis and who experienced what we call positive turnover. She was hired by one of the two companies on a full-time basis."

Table 2.4. *Full-time integration of a timeshare HR manager*

2.2.2. *The profiles of the various stakeholders*

Four stakeholders in the EG network have been characterized: the timeshare HR manager, the EG (as a structure), the company manager and finally the territory. Concerning the typical profile of the timeshare HR manager, there appears to be a convergence as to the skills required. In addition to the technical skills that are the basis of the HR profession, those relating to the players' ability to meet the challenges of an atypical professional context are highlighted: maturity, adaptability, organizational skills, listening skills, autonomy, etc. (Table 2.5).

MD-EG1	"It is much easier to teach someone who already has technical soft skills than a set of cross-cutting skills because they are created on a background of educational, sociological, experiential history."
MD-EG3	"If you don't have the professional maturity, timesharing is destructive."
EGM1	"You need people who have a professional project, who are good communicators, who are open-minded. It's important to communicate well with the different parties."
HRM1	"I think you have to be adaptable. Because we have three managers, three different personalities, a hundred employees. So you have to adapt each time."
SME1	"For small companies, it's an asset to no longer have this HR hat on, to have someone from the company who has this HR hat on and who can advise the manager. Who will also be able to listen to their employees."

Table 2.5. *The profile of the timeshare HR manager*

Expectations for the EG to develop provisions for the best conditions differ. For some actors, the EG has no vocation to interfere in the relationships that are established between the timeshare HR manager and the SME. Its first vocation would thus be a simple role of intermediary between the member companies, by expressing and listening to their needs, and the timeshare employees, through the detection and the development of competences which they will activate (Table 2.6). For others, the EG must above all be at the heart of the relationship, be the "pilot" actor of the network. This legitimacy to assume the role of pilot is discussed by a manager of an SME because of the lack of influence of this type of structure, whose organizational methods are still mostly unknown. To be a determining player for the various stakeholders would require a strong professionalization of support and network animation practices within EGs.

MD-EG1	"The radical thinking is to say no, you absolutely do not want to be a middleman, you want to be the alpha and omega of your relationships. And that position was a psychological revelation for the team."
EGM2	"The role appears to me as HR in the mediation side, but we are also an employer. But it's also our responsibility."
EGM2	"Very often managers don't perceive everything that is said to us. They don't even think about what the employee might say. But we are also very discreet about this. It's a raw material for us, to accompany the company. We hear things that will certainly be useful to us in our member and employee relationships."
SME1	"And this is also the difficulty of timesharing, to be entities known locally and only locally. […] In timesharing, if there was a larger timeshare company recognized in France, it would be important. They are small units in the end. It hurts timesharing."
HRM1	"For me, it doesn't interfere. It wouldn't occur to me to go look. I find it quite embarrassing. And even for them arriving saying 'she told me that …'. If I can't say it, I either don't say it, or I force myself, but it is with the leader."

Table 2.6. *Profiles of EGs*

The profile of the manager also influences the conditions of the timeshare HR manager's success, with a fairly good convergence in the comments of the actors met. For the EG and the timeshare employees, it is a question of measuring the manager's expectations in relation to a function that they are generally unfamiliar with and whose representation is very regularly based solely on the logic of cost (Table 2.7). The manager must therefore be open to the opportunities that integration of the HR function offers for the development of their company and for the exercise of their profession.

Beyond the characteristics of the different stakeholders, those concerning the territory in which a timeshare is deployed were often put forward by the actors interviewed as a strong element in the timeshare's success. It is possible to note, moreover, a convergence on those of the territory's characteristics that would be more favorable than others. Thus, the initiatives that gave rise to the creation of EGs emanate from companies anchored to their territory and concerned about basing their development on the pooling of skills. The territories investigated during this research would thus have attributes that allow for the creation and deployment of this mode of organization: "territories of trust", "territories of cooperation" (Table 2.8).

EGM2	"We have company executives who are clueless about human resources, who say, 'There are people who seem to know what they're talking about. Let's meet them'. There are others who see us as a good resource, a bit like a recruitment agency. And we have to be able to sort that out because if we are seen too much like that, it's not the point. There is going to be a predation of our employees that is going to be too fast."
EGM3	"It has to be a leader who wants to share, to have support for the strategy. It's true for a timeshare, but it's also true on a full-time basis. This pairing is the key to success for a company's HR position."
SME1	"These are functions that cost the company and which, I put in quotation marks, 'in theory', do not bring in anything […]. So you have to have the means to invest in this function because if you do it just to tell the person that it's to make pay slips, it's absolutely useless. That means that behind it, there are going to be other resources to be made available, training plans … It's all of that."
HRM1	"According to the manager profile, they have to give me material, confide in me, share their expectations and objectives. If I'm confined to doing paperwork in an office, it won't work."

Table 2.7. *Profiles of the leaders*

MD-EG1	"These are territories that have more confidence than others."
MD-EG1	"It's the proximity! All the real work has to happen on a life scale that doesn't go past half an hour. I'd even say ideally 15 minutes."
MD-EG3	"I think that here the practices of cooperation between companies, they are in the territory's DNA."
EGM1	"This territorial notion is important in creating a grouping. It's the companies in a given territory that are pilots, that want to support creation of a cluster."
HRM1	"I think that the notion of network is important. I have the impression that here in this basin there are quite a few people who think that it is important, that the territory must be kept alive. This is the basis of the organization of the employers' group."

Table 2.8. *Profiles of the territories*

2.2.3. *The nature and quality of relationships between the stakeholders*

For all the actors interviewed, the challenge of making the network work well involves building trust (Table 2.9).

MD-EG2	"The words 'trust' and 'responsibility' guide our management."
MD-EG1	"It's simple, when I was unhappy in a position, you were there. When I wanted to change, you were there. When I expressed very concrete training needs, you responded. Well, these are elements that I don't have elsewhere. You are my security."
EGM1	"And when we manage to have those relationships of trust, transparency, mutual respect, it works well."
SME1	"If you have someone you trust, it will always go well."
SME2	"When you are in a small family structure, it is difficult to delegate. [...] There's the trust part and the trust in the other person."
HRM1	"They [the leader] let me take care of it [the human]. So they have to trust me and I have to trust them too."

Table 2.9. *Trust between the parties*

If the convergence of the parties' interests is a condition of success for the network, it appears from our results that this point constitutes an element of fragility and complexity for the timeshare network (Table 2.10). The interest of integrating a timeshare HR manager is based, on the one hand, on the missions that are allocated to them. The expectations of both parties must be clearly re-formulated upstream and go beyond the mere administrative dimension. The interest of the parties must, on the other hand, relate to the modality of the timeshare. SME managers need to see the added value of pooling skills. If interest in resorting to this modality is based only on a duration adapted to the need of the company, the network appears quite fragile in the long run. A need that grows within the company results in an automatic transformation of the position to full time.

The durability of the timeshare network around the EG depends fundamentally on the emergence of a feeling of belonging among the stakeholders, the employees made available and the member companies. For the timeshare HR manager and the members, this feeling did not appear in our results (Table 2.11).

EGM1	"The employer grouping is very systemic. Everything fits together. But the interests of each are not necessarily convergent."
MD-EG3	"To make sure that they have understood, that we are sure of the commitment, the durability, the social ethics."
MD-EG1	"The whole relationship is swallowed up by something that is quite paradoxical. We promised a simple experience for the member, for the employee, but in reality, but in our actual experience, it's not simple at all."
MD-EG1	"We recently had a member tell us, and it was a revelation for us, 'But I have no interest in hiring someone full time at my place. What my two-day employee does, she'll never do full time at my place. Because, what she learns at Peter's or Paul's next door, I'll lose'."
SME1	"There are bridges through the employee who straddles two companies. This leads to an increase in skills. Conversations about working conditions. The difference. It compares."
HRM3	"There were times when I struggled to fit in, which is why it was interesting, and in fact the EG and I had discussed it, why it was interesting to have management that was really motivated by implementing the HR function and was willing to support it with employees."

Table 2.10. *A necessary convergence in the parties' interests*

An initial explanation for this situation is the nature of the tripartite relationship (EG, HR manager, SME), which encourages a relationship with a particular actor in the network. It is thus the feeling of belonging to the company that appears most often. The integration of the timeshare HR manager within the member companies is indeed perceived as a key to success. However, the timeshare HR managers interviewed considered that they had a very weak relationship with the EG. One timeshare HR manager (HRM2) said that she did not have a sense of belonging, but rather an "attachment" to the two different entities (EG, SME). The real challenge for EGs is therefore to strengthen the sense of belonging to their structure by developing appropriate HR practices (training, network meetings, new economic model, etc.) to support employees.

MD-EG1	"Some say 'being in the EG community is important to me'. Some say, 'Being a member of the EG makes sense'. But that's barely 10% of our members. Some employees have been there since the beginning, and say 'I'm really happy to be a timeshare and that's why I'm happy'. But that's the minority."
MD-EG3	"The sense of belonging is not a given. It's something we have to work on. Otherwise we can quickly set up a self-service system where the employee takes what they have to take and then voila!"
EGM1	"Employees quickly feel that they belong to their companies. For me, this is also a key to success. Our success is that when a third party enters the company they can't see the difference between the employees and the EG employee. For me, this is a success factor."
EGM2	"This is a position that we are tending to develop more and more. The fact that the employee feels more and more like an employee of the EG. And that their employer appears as the EG. And this role is legitimate. And I think it is well perceived. And then it's about doing it skillfully."
SME1	"We have always considered the timeshare as an employee of the company. For sure, if they are considered separate from their colleagues, it's complicated."
HRM2	"I don't have a sense of belonging. I have an attachment to the different entities. I like working in both structures. I really like my colleagues in both entities. But I don't actually feel like I belong to the companies. In the same way, I very much appreciate the conversations I can have with the EG and the initiatives they can have, especially to animate relationships between the employees of the EG, but I also feel a little detached from that."

Table 2.11. *Sense of belonging*

2.3. Conclusion

Based on the results of the qualitative analysis, several findings can be highlighted in relation to the questions posed from a theoretical perspective on the success of a network. First, we note that each stakeholder benefits from the existence of the timeshare network. For the HR manager, the diversity of the missions and the challenges associated with the SME context explain their commitment to this form of employment. For the SME manager, the interest in using timeshares is based on the availability of competences with a time and cost adapted to need. As a "pilot" actor in the network, the EG's mission is then to offer a differentiated service adapted to stakeholder different expectations. However, divergent interests can also be observed in the long term. Turnover, which translates into the integration of a full-time HR manager in one of the member companies, is a perfect illustration. While some view it positively, as it is perceived as a recognition of the HR role within the SME, others condemn it, insofar as it leads the network to disappear. This reflects the difficulty stakeholders have in reaching a "balanced and sustainable compromise" (Xhauflair et al. 2010, p. 311).

We also note a lack of common sense given to the network. It is at this level that the fragility of the timeshare network is most apparent. Each stakeholder gives the EG a role corresponding to its own needs. In other words, each party derives an advantage from the network for itself, without taking into consideration a common, explicit objective, which is nevertheless the basis of the very definition of a network (Assens and Courie-Lemeur 2014).

It is important to note that the sustainability of the network, or even its development, is not embedded in any representation of the network's success, other than the EG itself. The bond of trust between the stakeholders seems essential (Chedotel and Viviani 2016). But it remains insufficient. Beyond trust, the feeling of belonging to the timeshare network appears to be both essential and very difficult to establish. This is a key element for the EG's success: knowing how to create a new feeling of belonging in the work relationship, which does not correspond to any known norm or organization of work (Lethielleux 2018). The timeshare HR manager must feel first and foremost a member of the network, which does not appear to be a reality in the results of the qualitative analysis.

Nevertheless, there appears to be a convergence of perceptions on the territory's favorable characteristics. This last point qualifies the observations made previously. The initiative that led to the creation of the timeshare network emerges from the territory. The territorial anchoring of the actors in the timeshare network appears as a lever for developing the network. This observation, which is to act for the territory, is shared by the stakeholders. The results clearly show a convergence, with determining characteristics clearly identified by the actors, in a unanimous way. Thus, the territory seems to be able to play a federating role between the stakeholders, a role that is undoubtedly insufficiently exploited in the long term by the EGs.

Development of the territory, which was a common objective for all the EG stakeholders in our results, seems to today to be a track that is not highlighted enough for giving even more meaning to these territorial networks. As an extension, the institutional support of local bodies (local authorities, for example) could also support and strengthen EGs in the territories. Within EGs, the job of timeshare HR manager has a short existence (less than 3 years), with many cases of full-time integration in member companies. Further, if the goal of an often displayed EG is to maintain and develop full-time employment in the territory, this must be done within the framework of shared time and not within the framework of integrating the employee into the company. This, on a large scale, would jeopardize the network's very existence. The response to this risk and this difficulty involves valuing the EG as a performance lever linked to the principle of pooling skills, which is the source of greater efficiency. If this is particularly true for the job of HR manager on a timeshare basis, it also applies to this form of employment more generally.

Two avenues of managerial recommendations appear that contribute to the success of the timeshare network via EGs. First, it seems essential to work on the common, shared meaning of the network. This can be done by further accentuating the impact of the EG on the territory, the latter seeming to play a particularly unifying role. However, the impact of the network on companies and employees, which is not very visible today for some actors, must be considered further. This involves identifying the added value of the network for companies and for employees, in particular that linked to the pooling of skills (vs. the simple sharing – or breakdown – of time). This presupposes that EGs have the ability to offer a high added value service to support the employees made available and the member companies with real expertise.

The sustainability of the network should thus become a convergent criterion of success, a common objective, with added value equitably distributed among the stakeholders: timeshare HR manager, business managers, territory and EG. Second, it also seems essential to rethink the professional identity of timeshare employees in order to work on the feeling of belonging, which is currently lacking and can even be a source of confusion in the identity of employees. Linked to both companies and EGs, they seem to have the feeling of not belonging to anyone, at least not to their employer (the EG). It is useful to promote the innovative image of this form of employment to succeed in generating a professional identity of its own.

2.4. Appendix

Coding	Name of the function
MD-EG1	Managing director of the EG
MD-EG2	Managing director of the EG
MD-EG3	Managing director of the EG
EGM1	Employer group "stakeholder" manager
EGM2	Employer group "stakeholder" manager
EGM3	Employer group "stakeholder" manager
SME1	SME manager
SME2	SME manager
HRM1	HR manager – timeshare
HRM2	HR manager – timeshare
HRM3	HR manager – timeshare

Table 2.12. *List of interviewees*

Theme 1	Through the example of the timeshare HR manager, what are the visions of success for the timeshare network?	
Theme 2	What are the conditions for success	Stakeholder characteristics: EG manager; SME manager; timesharing HR manager
		The nature and quality of relationships: EG and SME; timesharing HR manager and EG; timeshare HR manager and SME manager; between stakeholders
		The prerequisites for setting up the network and timesharing practices
		The influences of the territory, the economic and social context
Theme 3	Through the example of the timeshare HR manager, what are the areas of improvement for the operation of the timeshare network?	

Table 2.13. *Themes addressed*

2.5. References

Assens, C. and Courie-Lemeur, A. (2014). De la gouvernance d'un réseau à la gouvernance d'un réseau de réseaux. *Question(s) de management*, 8, 27–36.

Boulanger, P. (1990). *Organiser l'entreprise en réseau*. Nathan, Paris.

Carluer, F. (2006). Réseaux d'entreprise et dynamiques territoriales : une analyse stratégique. *Géographie, économie, société*, 193–214.

CESE (2018). *Les groupements d'employeurs*. Les éditions des Journaux officiels, Paris.

Chedotel, F. (2004). Avoir le sentiment de "faire partie d'une équipe" : de l'identification à la coopération. *M@n@gement*, 7(3), 161–193.

Chedotel, F. and Viviani, J.L. (2016). Dynamiques et conditions des relations coopératives dans les réseaux. *Revue française de gestion*, 259, 71–81.

Colin, T. and Mercier, E. (2017). Le territoire : de nouvelles opportunités pour la fonction RH ? *Management et Avenir*, 95, 107–127.

Cromarias, A. (2012). Entreprendre la flexicurité au niveau "méso" dans les PMO : le rôle clé du porteur de projet. *Revue internationale PME*, 25(2), 13–39.

Ettiggoffer, D. and Van Beneden, P. (2000). *Mét@-organisations, les modèles d'entreprises créateurs de valeurs*. Village Mondial, Paris.

Géniaux, I. and Mira-Bonnardel, S. (2003). Le réseau d'entreprises : forme d'organisation aboutie ou transitoire. *Revue française de gestion*, 129–144.

Habhab-Rave, S. (2009). Stratégie des réseaux et compétitivité : le cas des PME/TPE tunisiennes. *Humanisme et Entreprise*, 291(1), 25–46.

Hobfoll, S.E. (1989). Conservation of resources: A new attempt at conceptualizing stress. *American Psychologist*, 44(3), 513–524.

Holmlund, M. and Törnoos, J.A. (1997). What are relationships in business networks? *Management Decision*, 35(4), 304–309.

Hommel, T. (2006). Paternalisme et RSE : continuités et discontinuités de deux modes d'organisation industrielle. *Entreprises et Histoire*, 45, 20–38.

Joyeau, A. and Poilpot-Rocaboy, G. (2014). Enjeux et perspectives du métier de Responsable Ressources Humaines à temps partagé : une réponse au besoin d'innovation en matière d'emploi ? *Revue internationale de gestion*, 39(1), 79–92.

Joyeau, A. and Poilpot-Rocaboy, G. (2016). Le réseau d'entreprises au service de l'emploi : le temps partagé comme solution aux pénuries d'effectifs et de compétences sur un territoire. In *Collaborations et réseaux : approches transversales en management*, Bironneau, L. and Viviani, J.L. (eds). PUR, Rennes.

Joyeau, A., Le Gall, S., Poilpot-Rocaboy, G. (2016). Le métier de responsable RH à temps partagé. In *Quels métiers RH pour demain ?*, Scouarnec, A. and Poilpot-Rocaboy, G. (eds). Dunod, Paris.

Joyeau, A., Le Gall, S., Poilpot-Rocaboy, G. (2017). Libérons les dirigeantes et les dirigeants de PME ! Le RRH à temps partagé comme levier de développement de l'entreprise et du territoire. In *Pour une GRH inspirante. Une réponse au DRH Bashing*, Barabel, M. (ed.). Eyrolles, Paris.

Joyeau, A., Le Gall, S., Poilpot-Rocaboy, G. (2018a). La fonction RH à temps partagé : une question de santé pour le dirigeant de PME ? *Management et Avenir*, 101(3), 61–82.

Joyeau, A., Le Gall, S., Poilpot-Rocaboy, G. (2018b). Dirigeant et DRH en PME : une double casquette difficile à porter ! *29ème Congrès de l'AGRH*.

Lambert, D.M. and Cooper, M.C. (2000). Issues in supply chain management. *Industrial Market Management*, 29, 65–83.

Lethielleux, L. (2017). Réseaux et nouvelles configurations RH territoriales : le rôle des groupements d'employeurs. *Management et Avenir*, 95, 171–188.

Lethielleux, L. (2018). Les groupements d'employeurs : vers un nouveau développement de la GRH territoriale ? *Gérer et Comprendre*, 132, 3–10.

Lethielleux, L. and André, C. (2018). Groupement d'employeurs et gestion des défaillances des TPE/PME : le syndrome de l'arroseur arrosé. *Recherches en sciences de gestion*, 128, 205–224.

Loufrani-Fedida, S. and Saint-Germes, E. (2018). L'engagement durable des parties prenantes dans une démarche de GRH territoriale : le cas de la GTEC de Sophia-Antipolis. *Revue de gestion des ressources humaines*, 110, 18–40.

Mandard, M. (2015). *Les réseaux interorganisationnels*. La Découverte, Paris.

Mercier, S. (2010). Une analyse historique du concept de parties prenantes : quelles leçons pour l'avenir ? *Management et Avenir*, 33, 142–156.

Smith, K., Carroll, S., Ashford, S. (1995). Intra- and inter-organizational cooperation: Toward a research agenda. *Academy of Management Journal*, 38(1), 7–23.

Thorelli, H. (1986). Networks, between market and hierarchy. *Strategic Management Journal*, 7, 37–51.

Torre, A. (2016). La figure du réseau : dimensions spatiales et organisationnelles. *Géographie, économie, société*, 18, 455–469.

Vilette, M.A. (2008). Gérer autrement les RH en PME : convergence entre Travail à Temps Partagé et TIC. *Management et Avenir*, 16(2), 47–65.

Xhauflair, V., Pichault, F., Maesschalk, M.F. (2010). Partenariats interorganisationnels et nouvelles formes de gouvernance : les conditions d'un compromis équilibré et pérenne. *Management et Avenir*, 33, 298–316.

3

Contributions of a Science and Technology Park (STP) to Inclusive Mobility for a Territory

The inhabitants of small- and medium-sized cities and rural communities suffer from a lack of efficient, reliable and multi-modal mobility solutions. The private car remains the most widely used means of travel (despite the cost of ownership and use) and the use of public transport (bus, regional train, tramway) remains very low despite numerous incentives (such as free travel for several categories of the population). For some populations (young people and precarious workers in particular), this lack of mobility, this precarious mobility (any person who encounters obstacles in daily life), can clearly impact their lives: dropping out of school, choice of orientation, access to employment, employability, social and cultural life, etc. Mobility is a determining factor in access to employment in the same way as training, housing and health (one French person in four has refused a job because of a lack of means to get there). In France, mobility has become the number one expense for a household (18% of the budget on average) ahead of food and housing.

These observations have contributed to the emergence of the concept of inclusive mobility, which aims to offer physically and financially accessible solutions to categories of populations excluded from access to mobility (people on low incomes, job seekers, precarious workers, the elderly, people with reduced mobility, etc.). "However, the notion of inclusive mobility also

Chapter written by Isabelle KUSTOSZ and Stéphane MEURIC.

induces a critical distancing from mobility considered as a social norm" (Cass et al. 2005; Fol and Gallez 2014). This detachment implies interdisciplinary public policies aimed at reducing the "all-mobility" approach in favor of renewed access to resources. Inclusive mobility cannot therefore be considered exclusively from the economic angle, which focuses on the cost of transport and access to employment, but must be considered from an empowering and collaborative angle, encouraging the participation of all stakeholders in the issues it raises.

Legislative measures reflect the challenges of mobility by adding cultural and social dimensions to its spatial dimension. This is the case in France with the LOM law (law no. 2019-1428 of December 24, 2019, on mobility), which aims to reduce territorial inequalities and contribute to territorial cohesion. Mobility does indeed appear to be a major component of an inclusive society if we refer to the European Commission's definition of inclusion:

> a process that ensures that people at risk of poverty and social exclusion are provided with the opportunities and resources to participate fully in economic, social and cultural life, and [...] guarantees them better participation in the decision-making processes that affect their lives and better access to their fundamental rights. (COM 2003, p. 9)

This is the context of our case study of the Transalley Science and Technology Park (STP), located in the Valenciennes region (Hauts-de-France) and dedicated to innovative and sustainable mobility. We propose to question the contribution of STPs to an inclusive territory beyond their role in supporting economic development based on the technological innovation attributed to them. Through the case of this STP, we propose to apprehend the contributions of STPs to the intelligence of a territory by going beyond strictly technocentric approaches to value the methods favoring the co-construction of a shared vision for a territory that takes into account issues of inclusion.

The chapter is developed in four parts. First, it presents the recent contributions in the literature on the roles of STPs and on territorial intelligence by insisting on the extension of the concept to social value and social and collaborative governance beyond the technological aspects. It then describes the case of the Transalley Science and Technology Park, before proposing elements for a characterization of its different types of contributions through the study of three embedded projects: a demonstration and experimentation track, the Institute of Mobility and Sustainable Transport and the Mobility Kiosk. The detailed analysis of these three projects dedicated to mobility, whose motivations and issues are different, makes it possible to distinguish different methods of interventions and to observe their convergences.

Finally, on the basis of this empirical work, the mobilization of theoretical frameworks makes it possible to interpret the field observations from the perspective of the contribution of the STP to the inclusive territory. The final part of this chapter discusses the contributions of our analysis by linking them to the issues of collaborative governance, capacity building among local actors and the evaluation of the social value of STPs.

3.1. Main contributions of the literature

In the context of the renewed interest in the organizational form of STPs – now institutionalized for four decades – we propose to situate ourselves at the crossroads between work on the roles and contributions of STPs and work on the intelligence of cities and territories.

3.1.1. Contributions regarding STPs from the literature

Several reviews of the literature on STPs have been published recently, which show that there has been an evolution in the understanding of their challenges. The abundant literature from the fields of economics, management and geography is essentially focused on their effects, in terms of positive externalities, business performance and economic development, that these groups of public and private actors collaborating on innovations resulting from university research are likely to generate.

It is interesting to note that this literature is in line with the extension of the contributions on the triple helix, which emphasizes the interactions between the public, universities and business. Thus, it reflects an increased interest in the participation of civil society alongside issues of technology and economic transfer. The quadruple helix reflects the irruption of concerns related to the intervention of citizens, users, consumers, etc. More broadly still, the prospect of a quintuple helix reflects the inclusion of environmental concerns in the dynamics of innovation (Leydesdorff 2012).

Beyond an approach aimed at identifying a model to be copied and exported, which has characterized a large number of publications, an interest is developing in local contexts and the complexity of innovation ecosystems. Of course, mainstream economic theories situate the challenges of STPs in terms of outputs facilitated by localized knowledge, the transfer of tacit knowledge and technological change. However, we should take into account the great heterogeneity of configurations (Amoroso and Hervas 2019), which contributes to interrogating the different contributions of STPs. As a result, questions are raised about the economic impact of STPs, which remains difficult to measure due to their diversity, the multitude of knowledge externalities and other possible effects that they generate in a highly complex ecosystem and, consequently, the partial nature of the evaluation methods used (Phan et al. 2005).

Describing the state of the art of the contributions regarding STPs, Lecluyse et al. (2019) note the large number of studies on inputs analyzed in terms of success factors (location, size of the region, financial resources and support, management, reputation, etc.) and on their impacts (on innovation, business creation, job creation, economic growth, local development, etc.), but above all they note that the smallest number of articles deal with their role of mediating between stakeholders and therefore their contribution to building collaborative networks. This role of mediator nevertheless makes it possible to initiate new avenues of research on their social and societal impacts, in particular.

As such, Fulgencio et al. (2016) specifically ask the question of evaluation not only of their economic impacts but also of their impacts in terms of social value. By working on the social value of innovation ecosystems (civic value, well-being, social capital, environment), they intend not only to emphasize the importance of the role of social actors within STPs (associations, communities, organizations, etc.) but also the social impact of STPs at two levels: for the benefit of the entrepreneurs and companies hosted as well as more broadly in the direction of the territory's populations (Fulgencio 2017).

Lee and Kim (2018), for their part, characterize STPs according to the skills of their managers and in particular those that consist of promoting bottom-up approaches and boundary spanning skills, i.e. the ability to cross existing boundaries between stakeholders. The recent literature on STPs thus seems to have a strong influence on the way in which they are managed. It seems to show an interest in the participation of civil society and in the mediating role of the STP considered as a facilitating organization.

3.1.2. *Intelligence of cities and territories: From ICT to capabilities*

This evolution of the literature on STPs is similar to that underway in the literature on smart cities and territories. From a vision of intelligence essentially based on the use of technologies, and in particular ICTs, we are in fact moving towards a definition of intelligence based on collaborative governance, participation in civil society and the development of community capacities. Initially, "intelligence" was a concept understood from the point of view of the role of ICT in the creation of services and products that contribute to improving the quality of life of users and the transformation of urban processes, but gradually it has been enriched by alternative visions that take into account citizen initiative, empowerment and the density and quality of the interactions at stake. The top-down approach motivated by financial and commercial logics, which rests on the use of technologies, is then questioned by a bottom-up approach based on the recognition of interactions co-constructing appropriate solutions. A middle way between these two approaches allows us to consider more specifically the roles of local initiative platforms that promote the collective intelligence of the actors involved in the sense of a local variation of the major societal challenges that cross society (Breuer et al. 2014).

Thus, among the components of the smart city, we can certainly note the technological factors and also the importance of institutional and human factors (Nam and Pardo 2011). The agendas for future research are therefore oriented towards smart governance in terms of innovative forms of collaboration and collaborative governance (Meijer and Rodríguez Bolívar 2016). Smart governance is considered to be based on the possibilities offered by digitalization to enhance collaborations, information and knowledge sharing, citizen engagement, openness and transparency. In view of the need to involve citizens and users in decisions that are supposed to improve the quality of life (Pereira et al. 2018), the intelligence of a city or territory can no longer be reduced to its digital dimension, which is supposed to facilitate access to data and its effect on new or optimized processes/products. It is therefore in the continuity of the developments just described that we analyze the case of the Transalley Science and Technology Park and its contributions to the inclusive territory.

3.2. Description of the Transalley case and its three embedded sub-cases

The Transalley Science and Technology Park, located in the extension of the Université polytechnique Hauts-de-France campus, aims to create innovative economic activity linked to research and higher education in the region. It is developing several functions, combining physical space with animation and support services: a business hotel, an incubator, a business accelerator and a mediation space for clusters. These various functions serve as a resource center for the entire mobility sector, particularly the automotive and rail sectors. Indeed, Transalley is a structural project for the Valenciennes region (Hauts-de-France) within the regional economic development plan, which supports the mobility clusters of the region. It thus contributes to the regional innovation strategy (SRI-SI[1]) on transport and ecomobility in the Hauts-de-France region. The STP supports the emergence of structuring projects, such as technological platforms, shared between the various stakeholders in a partnership approach.

The association responsible for the STP is developing its actions around three main areas: (1) raising awareness of business creation, detection, support for project leaders, accommodation for business creators and young companies; (2) supporting and strengthening the mobility sector, including the railway sector, the automotive sector, mobility services and niche activities relating to the mobility of goods and people; (3) promoting the sector by enhancing its players and assets (industrial, scientific, territorial, etc.) at the regional, national and international levels through representation and communication activities.

This chapter is based on an analysis of three interlocking projects, i.e. carried out simultaneously by the STP but which present differentiated objectives: the development of an experimentation and demonstration track intended to test connected smart roads; the event management of the Institute for Sustainable Mobility and Transport (IMTD) intended to support collective reflection on mobility issues; the Mobility Kiosk, and an action

---

1 Smart Specialization Strategy (S3).

program of the PIA program (a future investment program) focusing on inclusive mobility for young people in the area (13–30 years old). It is precisely through the theme of mobility that we examine the various types of contributions made by the STP to show how it has broadened its scope to include issues of inclusion. In addition, the articulation of these different types of contributions within the STP's project allows us to consider a dual approach to inclusion at the organizational and processual level, between social inclusiveness and partnership or collaborative inclusiveness.

3.2.1. Demonstration and experimentation track

The STP is providing regional players with an experimentation and demonstration track on the site to test connected smart roadways and new autonomous vehicles. This equipment represents an important link for the site's researchers, allowing them to carry out tests in real and secure conditions, as an extension of the work carried out in the laboratory. Different experimental configurations are possible, representing different uses (parking, vehicle/bike cohabitation, accessibility for people with disabilities and complex situations (traffic circles, interaction between roadways, communication signaling equipment and vehicles, etc.)).

In addition to research and development activities, this platform is used to provide training to students and professionals on various subjects in a safe environment. A supplementary use of the track is oriented towards the general public for promotion, road safety and ecomobility awareness actions. Indeed, the emergence of new forms of mobility (micromobility, urban mobility) has led to the appearance of new rolling machines and new practices (trotting, skateboarding, monowheeling, etc.), which raise issues of road safety and accidentology and also of cohabitation and sharing of spaces. Finally, as the track is at the heart of the STP, companies can use it to develop products and showcase new vehicles. As regards the latter use, its spatial situation favors the organization of events for the general public.

The characteristics of this track were defined upstream by carrying out several actions:

– The benchmarking of existing tracks in France and in the world. Over the last few years, several tracks have been built, even reconstituting entire cities.

– The collection and analysis of researchers' needs in terms of test typology and test configuration.

– The collection and analysis of the needs of car manufacturers, equipment manufacturers, new players in urban mobility (start-ups) and transport operators.

The main objective of the track is research and technological development, but it also offers uses oriented towards students, users and the general public, notably through training activities.

3.2.2. *Presentation of the Institute for Sustainable Mobility and Transport*

The Institute for Sustainable Mobility and Transport (*Institut des mobilités et des transports durables* (IMTD)) has different aspects. The institute was initially designed to promote the training and research work carried out by the university in the field of transport and mobility. Located at the interface of the campus and the STP, the IMTD is also a meeting place for the players in the ecosystem and provides the region with credibility as one of the main areas of smart specialization. In addition to its initial mission of opening up to the socio-economic world, particularly in the mobility sector (automotive, railways), the institute is also reaching out to employment and career guidance stakeholders to help them discover the potential of the sector. The institute also reaches out to the general public through scientific mediation and the promotion of scientific culture. It is thus a vector of attractiveness for local institutions, scientific and economic communities and the associative sector. Due to the hybrid nature of the site's uses and the audiences it welcomes, the IMTD is considered to be a place of welcome and exchange for the STP's and the region's ecosystem.

This institute has various modular spaces: documentation center, conference room, amphitheater, large exhibition area, creativity room, immersive room, fablab, research valorization area and reception area. Important work has been carried out with the teachers and researchers and also by analyzing and visiting other similar places with a view to comparison. The objective was to imagine new practices of promotion and communication around sustainable mobility. The IMTD's missions were thus expanded within the framework of its technopolitan governance. The interaction with cluster-type professional associations, STP companies, employment stakeholders and local authorities has revealed needs in terms of the attractiveness of professions, knowledge of the mobility industry and the need to better promote innovations, in particular. In order to organize all these events, a programming committee has been set up. It is made up of three colleges in the image of technopolitan governance: representatives of education and research, representatives of the socio-economic world and representatives of public institutions.

This place is therefore oriented towards the promotion of the sector, and also towards the participation of all the stakeholders of the territory in the collective reflection on mobility issues.

3.2.3. *Presentation of the Mobility Kiosk*

The territory has taken up the issue of inclusive mobility within the framework of a national call for projects (the *Agence nationale pour la rénovation urbaine* (ANRU), the French National Agency for Urban Renewal) by targeting youth through the "*accroche active*" program. The Mobility Kiosk (*Kiosque Mobilité*) is an action program on inclusive mobility within the framework of the investment program for the future – the PIA for youth (13–30 years). Its purpose is to raise awareness and train and support this group of people in order to increase their mobility as a means of integration and access to training and employment. The Mobility Kiosk is particularly active with young people: high school students, students, job seekers and precarious employees. It is an information point, promoting sustainable modes of transport and raising awareness of ecomobility and road safety. This is done through practical workshops using educational kits and role-playing. It offers individual diagnoses to the target public, so as to provide concrete solutions to the users of the territory. It offers mobility services such as the loan of electric vehicles, two-wheelers, scooters, etc.

The objective is to enable all young people in the region to access greater autonomy in terms of mobility and thus promote their access to training and employment more serenely and sustainably. This experimental operation is part of a dense ecosystem made up of administrations, public and private actors in the fields of employment, integration, training and pre-existing mobility operators. The kiosk's offer is deliberately positioned on a cross-cutting approach. The Mobility Kiosk program was designed on the basis of a territorial diagnosis: the profiles of young people (dropouts, unemployed, etc.), access to training and higher education, the employment rate, material conditions, precariousness and mobility, etc.

The Mobility Kiosk therefore offers inclusive mobility actions and services in partnership with other local actors and provides an integrated approach that allows a beneficiary to have a complete vision of what mobility covers (use, sector, employment, technology, innovation, access to a variety of resources, etc.).

3.3. Elements for characterizing the contributions of the STP

Our analysis was conducted on the basis of documentary studies (calls for projects and responses to calls for projects, internal working documents, communication documents, etc.) and direct observations (meetings, committees, etc.). It is based on empirical and epistemic work grounded in both the description and understanding of situations through access to local knowledge, as well as in reflexivity fed by a back and forth with the literature and concepts (Albert and Avenier 2011).

Nature of the project	Tracking specific equipment dedicated to the tests of innovative mobility	Institute event-based programming: a space for mediation and popularization	Kiosk program: awareness and actions
Project issues	– Offering to the actors of innovation a place for R&D experiments and trials – Serving as living labs – Raising awareness of technological innovations among target audiences	– Showing – Disseminating – Communicating – Networking	– Making the target populations more mobile, particularly with a view to employability – Optimizing the employment pool through mobility
Target audience/users	– Companies for their R&D component – The actors in research and training – Open to users	– Actors of the entrepreneurial ecosystem – General public	Young people between the ages of 13 and 30 (high school students, students, job seekers)

Actions taken	– Experimentation on technological products and new mobility solutions – Appropriation behaviors (traffic scenarios, etc.)	– Project codesign – Debating around societal issues and challenges – Organization conferences, workshops, exhibitions, projections, etc.	Putting into practice the uses (application, etc.)
Partners	Innovation actors (large groups, SMEs, start-ups, foundations, competitiveness or excellence clusters, communities of entrepreneurs)	Institutional actors of the ecosystem and the attractiveness of the territory	– Mobility actors – Associations – Local, regional and national governments – Actors in local multi-year plans for integration and employment
Carrying out the project	Co-sponsorship by the agglomeration community and the university	University co-sharing (real estate) and STP (uses)	Coordination by the STP
Registration in a national, regional or local program	– Smart Specialization Strategy (S3) of the FEDER – Sectors of excellence and competitiveness clusters – Strategic axes of the university	– ERDF (management of interdisciplinary projects) – CSTI (national strategy for scientific, technical and industrial culture)	– Youth future investment program – *Agence nationale pour la rénovation urbaine* (ANRU, National Agency for Urban Renewal)
Origin of funds	– European Regional Development Fund (ERDF) – National Planning and Development Fund of the Territory (FNADT) – Support Fund for Local Investment (FSIL)	Campus Plan 2008 State – Region	ANRU, community of agglomeration

Table 3.1. *Characteristics of the three embedded projects*

3.3.1. *Characteristics of the three observed projects*

We produced an observation grid for the three projects, allowing us to differentiate between them in terms of their nature, orientation and objectives, their target audiences and users, the actions they implement, the partners they involve and their institutional support, their inclusion in a national, regional or local strategy and the origin of the funds (Table 3.1).

In all three projects, in addition to the functions generally attributed to STPs in terms of support for technological innovations, we observed the implementation of activities and the inclusion of mechanisms aimed at developing broader networks and supporting the capacities of local actors, both stakeholders and users/citizens. In addition to the innovation and entrepreneurship players, who are generally associated with the activities of an STP, the general public and the target public concerned by precariousness and mobility, as well as associations and integration players, are also involved.

3.3.2. *Contributions of the STP through the three projects*

On the basis of these descriptive characteristics, it seems appropriate to distinguish the contributions of the STP according to three main types of interventions: technocentric interventions aimed at developing technologies, particularly in relation to the creation of opportunities; collaborative interventions aimed at developing interactions between stakeholders in the context of a common project; and finally capacity-building interventions aimed at developing the capacities of local actors, citizens and users. Our main contribution is thus to identify three types of orientation in the interventions of the STP:

– technology-oriented intervention (supporting technological innovation);

– intervention oriented towards collaborations (supporting the collective project at the territory level);

– capacity-oriented intervention (capacity-building role aimed at users/citizens).

	Technology-oriented	Collaboration-oriented	Capability-oriented
Test track and experimentation	*Organizing all types of tests concerning smart mobility (autonomous vehicles, smart urban furniture, signage, traffic regulation, etc.)*	Developing the local network of collaborations between research laboratories, start-ups and companies	– Living lab for the development of user capabilities (road safety, economical driving, use of applications, etc.) – Bottom-up approach to collect data and information from different stakeholders
Institute for Sustainable Mobility and Transport	– Showroom of innovations – Dissemination and debate around technological innovations, their impact and acceptability	*– Developing the legitimacy of the public–private stakeholder sector by making visible the specialization of the territory* *– Initiating hybrid projects and collaborative opportunities*	– Creating meaning, shared vision and responsibility – Sharing a common vision of mobility issues concerning the territory – Boundary spanning, boundary openers
Mobility Kiosk	– Informing users/citizens about technological innovations – Promoting new sustainable mobility	Coordinating the activities of local authorities and all stakeholders in the framework of youth mobility	*– Encouraging the emergence of new behaviors, skills and habits in users-citizens* *– Contributing to employability and well-being through mobility*

Table 3.2. *Contributions of the STP according to its orientations*

However, while each has a dominant focus (shown in italics in Table 3.2), these three types of interventions are not watertight in relation to each other. By questioning the technological, collaborative and facilitating contributions of the STP, we offer the possibility of a discussion to articulate these three orientations in the direction of a renewed governance that favors the development of smart, even inclusive, territories: strict technocentric approaches are overcome in order to support territorial intelligence between stakeholders and on the basis of the interactions that underpin it. The technopolitan project, which is part of a shared territorial project for mobility, is based on the complementarity of technopolarized, collaborative and enabling approaches.

Transalley's various forms of action show that the technocentric approach at the origin of an STP project can be complemented by objectives of animation of the territory (in the sense of scientific mediation aimed at a broad public or attractiveness for local institutions and scientific organizations), as well as by an approach of inclusion in favor of different publics. In all three cases, it is the participation of local stakeholders (institutional, business, scientific, users) that the STP organizes and optimizes, which gives a smart dimension to the projects carried out, to the resulting achievements and to the territory in which they are located.

Going beyond the technological and entrepreneurial functions (innovation, incubation, establishment and creation of companies) of STPs remains to be discussed from the perspective of their other functions and in order to situate the smart territory at the crossroads between technologies, collaborations and capacities.

3.4. From a smart territory to an inclusive territory

In this section, our discussion revolves around the following three questions:

– An STP promotes collaborative processes by contributing to the construction and dissemination of a shared vision of the territory: can mobility be considered as a common good around which the actors of the territory collaborate?

– The STP, beyond its technological orientation and the cohesive approach it encourages, proposes inclusive actions: can the STP be considered as an organization enabling organization for the stakeholders and the populations concerned?

– Finally, on the basis of these different contributions, the activities of the STP are difficult to evaluate: is it possible to assess the activity of the science park in terms of its social value?

In particular, our discussion shows the links between social inclusion and collaborative governance. By assuming a collaborative leadership extended to all stakeholders, STPs, through their various contributions, are likely to include in collaborative arrangements all those who are concerned by a problem and who can participate in its formulation and mediation.

3.4.1. *Collaborations and territory project*

Any collaborative process is based on building trust, empowering stakeholders (mutual recognition of their interdependence, intellectual property rules, etc.) and on the shared comprehension of issues and problems (common definition, common values). The STP, as a hybrid mediation structure, contributes to articulating different institutional logics in the direction of a shared project to improve collaboration between stakeholders. It combines technological and social dynamics by supporting a common vision of the territory (Kustosz 2017).

In the case studied, the STP promotes a perception of mobility as a common good for the territory shared by public actors, companies, universities, associations and users. As an interface structure between public authorities, the market and civil society, the STP supports, on the basis of this shared perception, a participatory dynamic that enables escaping the framework of competition between actors that the theory of rational choice favors. The open innovation theory (Chesbrough 2006) is generally called upon to understand the interest that stakeholders find in collaborating with each other on market-oriented technological innovation issues and the way in which this well-understood interest is based on highly structured intellectual property rights.

However, what the open innovation theory neglects is the engagement and responsibility for the territory that can be shown by the various stakeholders concerned. Hence, we propose to use Ostrom's (1990) approach, which can be used to understand the ins and outs of collaborative governance, both for its contributions to polycentric organization and the management of common goods. The concept of polycentricity makes it possible to understand how complex coordination processes are conducted between actors with heterogeneous points of view, values and capacities for action, considering that the diversity of decision-making centers generates added value rather than chaos.

This collaborative governance, which promotes the quality of relations between local actors, is based on the engagement of the actors with collective action, trust and reciprocity. It is by participating in the perception of mobility as a common good that the STP contributes to this engagement. The commons – as a third way between the State and the market – makes it possible to think about the production of knowledge and its sharing, the impact on the organization of activities and on the relations between stakeholders, by highlighting new power relationships that are not based solely on ownership, but rather on collaboration. As a structure carrying interactions oriented by a territorial project, and more particularly a regional strategy based on smart specialization (Nauwelaers et al. 2014), the STP not only opens up opportunities for collaboration between the innovation actors concerned but also other possibilities aimed more broadly at other actors ranging from politicians and associations to citizen-users. To do this, it completes the range of services intended for companies with communication actions, the organization of meetings and debates, as well as event operations. It therefore enhances not only the technological capital of the territory, but also its social capital (networks, associations, standards, values, etc.), which allows better cooperation for a common and collective benefit in the direction of the general interest.

This role of supporting the territory's project and the smart specialization strategy (S3) can certainly be considered as contributing to the collaborative management of a common good for the territory, yet it can also be considered in a more trivial way as a simple branding of the territory. The boundary between territorial project and territorial marketing, as well as between empowerment and the customer value proposition, seems difficult to define. In the same way, the collaborative governance set up must be questioned. For the time being, it essentially brings together public bodies (municipalities and agglomeration communities), university actors (universities and laboratories) and associations of professionals in the sector. It also relies on partnerships with other players in the employment and integration. What is really happening with the participation of the latter and of users/citizens in the collaborative governance of the STP? It is therefore necessary to further analyze the role of the STP in the animation of participatory mechanisms.

3.4.2. *Organization and inclusive approach on two levels*

Mobility issues can be considered according to a socio-technical approach at the crossroads between digitalization, which optimizes access to useful data for entrepreneurial actors via ICTs, and constructive interactions, which allow for the development of an intelligence of uses, i.e. an appropriation of the environment through practices. It is also possible, even further, to question the inclusive dimension of mobility as supported by the STP. Around a theme such as mobility, the animation and stimulation of links with associations and public structures in charge of inclusion are essential for the STP.

The definition of inclusion can be understood according to four dimensions of participation in society: the consumption dimension (having the power to buy), the production dimension (not being unemployed, working), the civic engagement (right to vote, participation in associations) and finally that of social interactions (integration into family, friend and community networks) (Damon 2008). Generally, inclusion is understood as the opposite of exclusion, i.e. in favor of the most vulnerable who are inhibited by their economic and social situation in the elementary functioning guaranteeing autonomy and freedom of choice (Sen 1999). However, we propose to understand it more broadly as the participation of all the actors of the territory in the sense of an increased collective capacity, whether organizational, entrepreneurial, etc. It is therefore not only a question of taking an interest in the action of the STP in favor of the capabilities of the populations of a territory, i.e. the realization of their functions, but also the strategic and organizational capacities of territorial organizations, in the sense of participatory inclusiveness based on an institutional model in favor of collaborative governance (Ansell and Gash 2008). These two approaches are in any case linked. Kourtit et al. (2012) underline that smart governance concerns proactive and open-minded governance structures that involve all actors in order to maximize the socio-economic and ecological performance of cities and cope with negative externalities and developed path dependencies.

Considering the STP as an empowering organization, this site, in our opinion, not only analyzes the scope of its actions in terms of empowerment, but, more broadly, of learning and interorganizational collaborations supported by mechanisms for sharing knowledge and skills. The empowering organization is notably based on pluralism (recognition of the diversity of purposes), participation (discussions around purposes and means of implementation), development (possibility of converting opportunities into value realizations) and responsibility (integrating a social dimension) (Vero and Zimmerman 2018).

In the same way that care must be taken to distinguish between collective action in favor of the territory and territorial marketing, it is also advisable, with regard to the participation of local actors, not to confine oneself to mechanisms that aim to promote the social acceptability of technical innovations, but to identify mechanisms that genuinely enable the development of the capacities of local actors. The capacity to act technically, like a citizenship that is not political but technical, makes it possible to reintroduce contingency into technological domains that are often imposed on users as undisputable facts (Feenberg 2014). As such, collaborative governance of STPs still needs to be expanded beyond the usual configuration of universities/labs/public actors.

3.4.3. Evaluation of STP activity by social value

According to our analysis, STPs offer contributions not only in terms of economic gains and entrepreneurial dynamics but also in terms of a range of public values (Landry 2006). To do so, they propose an integrative leadership that is likely to create public value by exploiting the potentials and fertilizing the skills of the actors in the territorial ecosystem. However, the broadening of STP contributions that we have just highlighted raises the question of the evaluation of their action. The financial and institutional support of STPs by certain stakeholders is based on an expectation of convincing results that justify the investment made.

The STP generally has internal or governance-defined indicators to monitor its own development and impact. Among its most commonly used indicators, we find – whether in terms of number, amount, ratio – those linked to the creation of innovative companies (projects detected in laboratories; students and researchers made aware; projects in incubation; companies created, accelerated, established, etc.), those related to partnership projects (research collaborations, patent filings, etc.), those related to structuring projects (joint laboratories, technological platforms, training, etc.), those related to the development of the park as a real estate operation (built buildings, marketing of spaces, etc.) and those related to the supply of services to companies (tertiary, technological expertise, access to shops, etc.). The STP also consolidates, on the scale of its territory of action and within the framework of the companies it supports, the number of jobs created, the percentage of turnover devoted to R&D, international operations, investment share, etc.

In addition to these quantified outputs in terms of economic activity, entrepreneurship and technological innovation, or even operations, there are, however, second-level effects that are generally more difficult to measure and therefore less used. We have seen that the opening up to actors in the fields of employment, integration, vocational training, scientific culture, etc., leads to new actions that have yet to be identified in order to be evaluated. In the same way, taking into account target audiences – more broadly, users or even the general public – requires evaluating their participation and the levels of appropriation, autonomy and capacity for action that it generates. It seems important to mobilize elements and criteria for a more integrative evaluation that takes into account not only the added value of the interactions fostered by the STP but also the level of adherence of the actors to the territorial project, as well as the development of the capacities of users-citizens and local actors.

As studies on STPs, generally devoted to their economic and technological orientation, are gradually evolving towards taking into account their production of public value (Moore 1995), it is therefore appropriate to question the way in which STPs create this public value in the context of territorialized action.

3.5. Conclusion

Through this case, we have shown that the activities of the STP can go far beyond the economic, technological and entrepreneurial orientations that are generally attributed to it to cover a cohesive and inclusive approach on a territory of action. We have studied three projects embedded within the Transalley case study – a demonstration and experimentation track, the Institute of Mobility and Sustainable Transport and the Mobility Kiosk – and we have shown that each of these projects has an inclusive dimension for the territory – even though their dominant focus is on technological development, the development of collaborations and the development of the capacities of local actors.

This broadening of the STP's contributions is favored by its theme of mobility. Through this specific theme, the STP supports, from a cohesive perspective, a territorial project experienced as a common good by the territorial actors, which guarantees their collaboration and participates, in an inclusive perspective, in the development of the capacities of local actors. We have thus proposed to conceive inclusion two different aspects: the inclusion of the most precarious, which aims at the opportunities to realize their own choices (as it is most often understood), and participatory inclusiveness, which associates the actors of the territory around a cohesive project (in the sense of the appropriation of a territorial project by many diversified actors). In doing so, we contribute to defining the intelligence of the territory, understood in its collaborative and inclusive dimension and not only technologically.

However, in order to reach a certain level of generalization, our analysis must be enriched by a multi-case approach that can compare different science and technology parks with different themes (materials, nanotechnologies, textiles, health, etc.). It would then be appropriate to use these other cases to assess their contribution to the inclusive territory not only through the degree of openness of their governance but also in terms of their multi-dimensional and multi-public approach, which translates into extra-economic actions whose scope seems to be changing.

3.6. References

Albert, M.N. and Avenier, M.J. (2011). Légitimation des savoirs élaborés dans une épistémologie constructiviste à partir de l'expérience de praticiens. *Recherches qualitatives*, 30(2), 22–47.

Amoroso, S. and Hervas, F. (2019). An international perspective on science and technology parks. In *Science and Technology Parks and Regional Economic Development. An International Perspective*, Amoroso, S., Link, A.N., Wright, M. (eds). Palgrave MacMillan, New York.

Ansell, C. and Gash, A. (2008). Collaborative governance in theory and practice. *Journal of Public Administration Research and Theory*, 18, 543–571.

Breuer, J., Walravens, N., Ballon, P. (2014). Beyond defining the smart city. Meeting top-down and bottom-up approaches in the middle. *TeMA – Journal of Land Use, Mobility and Environment* [Online]. Available at: https://www.researchgate.net/publication/307795127_Beyond_Defining_the_Smart _City_Meeting_Top-Down_and_Bottom-Up_Approaches_in_the_Middle.

Cass, N., Shove, E., Urry, J. (2005). Social exclusion, mobility and access. *The Sociological Review*, 53(3), 539–555.

Chesbrough, H. (2006). Open innovation: A new paradigm for understanding industrial innovation. In *Open Innovation: Researching a New Paradigm*, Chesbrough, H., Vanhaverbeke, W., West, J. (eds). Oxford University Press, Oxford.

COM (2003). 773 final. Joint report on social inclusion summarising the results of the examination of the national action plans for social inclusion (2003–2005), communication from the Commission to the Council, the European Parliament, the European Economic and Social Committee and the Committee of the Regions.

Damon, J. (2008). *L'exclusion*. PUF, Paris.

Feenberg, A. (2014). Technique et agency. *Revue du MAUSS*, 43(1), 169–180.

Fol, S. and Gallez, C. (2014). Social inequalities in urban access: Better ways of assessing transport improvements. In *Getting There/Being There: Financing Enhanced Urban Access in the 21st Century City*, Sclar, E., Lönnroth, M., Wolmar, C. (eds). Routledge, New York.

Fulgencio, H.T. (2017). Social value of an innovation ecosystem: The case of Leiden Bioscience Park, the Netherlands. *International Journal of Innovation Science*, 9(4), 355–373.

Fulgencio, H.T., Orij, D.R., Le Fever, D.H. (2016). Mapping and conceptualizing the measurement of organizational social value using systems thinking. *European Public and Social Innovation Review*, 1(1), 17–31.

Kourtit, K., Nijkamp, P., Arribas, D. (2012). Smart cities in perspective – A comparative European study by means of self-organizing maps. *Innovation: The European Journal of Social Science Research*, 25(2), 229–246.

Kustosz, I. (2017). Vers une gouvernance territorialisée de l'innovation : la participation de la sphère entrepreneuriale dans le cas de la spécialisation intelligente des régions. *Revue politiques et management public*, 34(1/2), 121–145.

Landry, C. (2006). *The Art of City Making*. Routledge, New York.

Lecluyse, L., Knockaert, M., Spithoven, A. (2019). The contribution of science parks: A literature review and future research agenda. *Journal of Technology Transfer*, 44(2), 559–595.

Lee, K.J. and Kim, E.Y. (2018). A leadership competency model of science and technology parks: The case of Chungbuk Techno Park in Korea. *Journal of Technology Management and Innovation*, 13(4), 105–114.

Leydesdorff, L. (2012). The triple helix, quadruple helix, ... and an N-tuple of helices: Explanatory models for analyzing the knowledge-based economy? *Journal of Knowledge Economy*, 3, 25–35.

Meijer, A. and Rodríguez Bolívar, M.P. (2016). La gouvernance des villes intelligentes. Analyse de la littérature sur la gouvernance urbaine intelligente. *Revue internationale des sciences administratives*, 82(2), 417–435.

Moore, M.H. (1995). *Creating Public Value: Strategic Management in Government*. Harvard University Press, Cambridge.

Nam, T. and Pardo, T.A. (2011). Conceptualizing smart city with dimensions of technology, people, and institutions. *Proceedings of the 12th Annual International Conference on Digital Government Research*.

Nauwelaers, C., Kleibrink, A., Stancova, K. (2014). The role of science parks in smart specialisation strategies. Report EUR 26701 EN, S3 policy brief series 08/2014, Publications Office of the European Union, JRC90719.

Ostrom, E. (1990). *Governing the Commons: The Evolution of Institutions for Collective Action*. Cambridge University Press, New York.

Pereira, G.V., Parycek, P., Falco, E., Kleinhans, R. (2018). Smart governance in the context of smart cities: A literature review. *Information Polity*, 23(2), 143–162.

Phan, P.H., Siegel, D.S., Wright, M. (2005). Science parks and incubators: Observations, synthesis and future research. *Journal of Business Venturing*, 20, 165–182.

Sen, A. (1999). *Development as Freedom*. Oxford University Press, Oxford.

Vero, J. and Zimmermann, B. (2018). À la recherche de l'organisation capacitante : quelle part de liberté dans le travail salarié ? *Savoirs*, 47(2), 131–150.

4

Understanding the Development of Social Enterprise in South Korea

The development of social enterprise is a relatively recent phenomenon that began to be studied in the Western context in the mid-1990s, at roughly the same time in Europe and the United States. The social enterprise concept was constructed and developed under this double influence, first in its two original contexts, where these two influences often combined, and then spread fairly widely in other contexts, where these two influences were enriched with elements specific to each of these contexts. National comparisons show that social enterprise has become an important player in inclusion in a territory, capable of providing original and adapted responses, most often in conjunction with national or local public policies and measures aimed in particular at the professional integration of unemployed people or people in categories of difficulty and/or the production of social services for the benefit of these people (Spear and Bidet 2005; Nyssens 2006; Kerlin 2013). Asia, and particularly South Korea, is one of the new contexts in which the social enterprise has gained traction in the past 15 years or so (Bidet and Defourny 2019). The craze for the social enterprise model is shared by actors from various backgrounds. In some Asian countries, it has generated a particularly complex ecosystem and very varied forms of social enterprise.

This chapter begins by reviewing the dual theoretical and geographical foundation on which the concept of social enterprise was built (section 4.1). It then presents the methodology adopted to carry out this research in South

Chapter written by Éric BIDET.

Korea (section 4.2) and proposes a typology of the main forms of social enterprise identified (section 4.3). Finally, it details the main results that this approach leads to highlighting and the main observations that can be drawn from it based on the ideal EMES type[1] as a reference model (section 4.4).

4.1. The concept of a social enterprise: A dual theoretical and geographical basis

The concept of a social enterprise emerged in the 1990s, building on the work of two research traditions that emerged in the 1970s: the non-profit model and the social economy model. The first was initially built on the observation of specific enterprises – foundations and associations in the Anglo-Saxon context; the other was built more on the analysis of European experiences strongly inspired by the cooperative model and the idea of a set of principles common to cooperative, mutual and associative enterprises.

The non-profit organization (NPO) model began to attract considerable academic interest in the 1980s with the work of Weisbrod (1978, 1988), Hansmann (1980), Young (1983), James and Rose-Ackerman (1986), Powell and Steinberg (1987) and Drucker (1990). From these first theoretical formalizations rooted in the study of the North American terrain, the project led by Johns Hopkins University in the early 1990s represented a turning point by extending this North American perspective to other geographical contexts (Salamon and Anheier 1996).

The approach adopted in this study was based on a methodology designed to have all the associated researchers validate a common set of criteria for belonging to the non-profit sector that could transcend national differences, so that this model could then be disseminated to other countries. Twelve countries from different backgrounds were thus involved in the initial phase (1992–1994) to reach a consensus on the criteria to be met: for an organization to be considered a non-profit organization, it must be (1) formalized, (2) private, (3) autonomous, (4) subject to rules of

---

1 EMES is the acronym used by an academic network working on social enterprise. This acronym originated from a research project entitled *L'Emergence de l'entreprise sociale en Europe i*("Emergence of Social Enterprise in Europe"), which brought together researchers from a dozen European countries in the second half of the 1990s. Their work led them to propose a typical ideal of the social enterprise, that is, an abstract model synthesizing the main characteristics of the social enterprise.

non-distribution of its surplus and (5) open to voluntary membership. The criteria identified by the study were used in 2006 by the United Nations to develop a nomenclature specific to the non-profit sector: the International Classification of Non-Profit Organisation (ICNPO). In its latest version (2017), this nomenclature has been extended beyond the non-profit sector stricto sensu by integrating other forms of private organizations that are primarily oriented towards the general interest while having a very limited distribution of profits (the case of certain cooperatives, in particular).

It is in the wake of this growing interest in the NPO model that the notion of social enterprise has emerged in the United States to reflect the capacity and the need for many NPOs to find market resources in response to the decline in their non-market resources. The notion of social enterprise thus appeared in 1993 at Harvard University on the initiative of Austin and Ragan, who founded the Social Enterprise Initiative, which was followed by the development of several studies and training programs oriented towards the management of NPOs. This interest, which quickly spread to other American universities, generated one of the first attempts to formalize the theory of the social enterprise model by Dees (1996), which would inspire numerous works in the following decades; in particular, those of Dart (2004), Nicholls (2006), Alter (2007), Young (2007), Light (2008) and Kerlin (2013).

In addition to its roots in the study of the NPO model, this approach to social enterprise is characterized by the close link it emphasizes with social innovation. It is also characterized by its emphasis on the figure of the social entrepreneur, their dynamism and ability to mobilize market resources to provide new and original responses to social needs. However, it does not pay particular attention to the social dimension linked to the governance model. It is historically disconnected from the cooperative model, which the analysis of NPOs does not initially include in its scope. In a context marked by the residual development of public social policy (liberal regime in Esping-Andersen's typology; public social spending below 20% of GDP in OECD studies) and a more pronounced orientation towards individualism, innovation and risk (according to the dimensions of culture identified by Hofstede), the Anglo-Saxon social enterprise is seen more as a new form of entrepreneurship which can be an effective substitute for public policies and as part of a strategy to reduce or control public spending, rather than as an element of a new type of public/private partnership or as a model that can inspire the renovation or renewal of public policies.

It was also in the first half of the 1990s that an interest in the social enterprise model emerged in Europe. This led to the creation in 1996 of the EMES network, bringing together researchers and research centers from different European Union countries. The approach adopted by EMES is inspired by the concept of social economy, which has its roots in experiences that appeared in the 19th century (Gueslin 1998; Ferraton 2007; Boutillier 2009) and which has been institutionally constructed in Europe since the 1980s (Chaves and Monzon 2012; Duverger 2016) by relying largely on the theoretical level on works such as those by Desroche (1976) and Vienney (1981), which initially focused on the cooperative model.

From the perspective promoted by EMES, social enterprise primarily embodies an extension of the model of the social economy enterprise in new directions and/or according to new methods but based on the same fundamental principles. The founding approach associated a dozen European countries engaged in a comparative research project that led to the identification of a base of criteria constituting an "ideal type of social enterprise" in Europe (Borzaga and Defourny 2001). These criteria are organized into three groups reflecting three dimensions specific to the European social enterprise: three criteria reflect the economic dimension of the social enterprise (having a continuous production activity, having a significant level of economic risk, having at least one paid job); three criteria reflect its social dimension (having an explicit objective of service to the community, being the result of an initiative from a group of citizens, adopting rules limiting or prohibiting the distribution of profits); three criteria reflect its democratic dimension (having a high degree of autonomy, adopting a decision-making process not based on the ownership of capital, having participatory governance involving the main parties concerned by the activity). In this approach, social enterprise is analyzed with reference to a model of collective enterprise characterized by rules of distribution of power which express collective governance and rules of distribution of surpluses and guarantee that these are mainly, even entirely, collectivized.

The ideal type defined by EMES is strongly inspired by the social cooperative model that appeared in Italy in the 1980s and was legally recognized in 1991. In a European context marked by long-standing and well-developed public social policies (Bismarckian and Beverid models, social-democratic and corporatist regimes in the Esping-Andersen typology; public social spending often exceeds 20% of GDP in OECD studies) and by national cultures more oriented towards respect for authority, moderate individualism and more risk aversion (according to the dimensions of culture identified by Hofstede), this European conception of social enterprise refers mainly to enterprises with democratic or participatory governance, which often operate in conjunction with public policies or mechanisms (particularly in the fields of integration through economic activity, services for the elderly and care for young children). As a result, they are often characterized by a "resource mix" made up of market resources (income from the sale of services or products), non-market resources (grants or donations) and non-monetary resources (volunteer work). The latter has often been interpreted as an element that guarantees the autonomy of these enterprises vis-à-vis the market and/or public authorities.

To an Anglo-Saxon conception that focuses on the skills and flair of the individual entrepreneur, social innovation and the market's capacity to respond to social problems corresponds a European conception which is more focused on the ability of collective entrepreneurship to renew and/or contribute to public policies and the emergence of a new private/public partnership in the social field. The two concepts, which emphasize different elements and sometimes divergent motivations to promote a similar entrepreneurial model – that of the social purpose enterprise – have spread widely since their formalization in the 1990s. They have influenced each other and also influenced other conceptions of social enterprise specific to the characteristics of each context. As the International Comparative Social Enterprise Models (ICSEM) project has undertaken to document since 2013, these notions have also served to name and bring together diverse experiences in most regions of the globe (Bidet and Defourny 2019; Gaiger et al. 2019), including in South Korea.

4.2. Methodology of the study

South Korea is a particularly interesting case study because it is economically close to, but socially and culturally very different from, Western countries. The country has a PPP GDP and HDI close to that of a country like France and a social protection system that is much more ambitious and protective than that of the United States. After having chosen to leave the resolution of social issues to economic growth alone during the 1960s and 1980s, Korea has developed its social protection system since the 1990s, even though the share of public social spending in GDP (at around 10%) still places the country in the lowest rankings within the OECD.

In this context, social enterprise has become a central element of employment, social services and community development issues over the past 15 years, leading to the establishment of a sophisticated and dynamic ecosystem for the promotion of social enterprise, which has found institutional recognition in Korea that is unprecedented in Asia to date.

It was during the 2006–2008 period that the concept of social enterprise became really visible in Korea in the scientific, political and media spheres. In order to analyze the development and transformations of this concept, we first examined documents of different statuses (academic articles, institute reports, legislative texts, activity reports of organizations, etc.). We then confronted and refined the experiences and arguments thus identified during meetings and field visits with some of the main actors in the Korean social enterprise ecosystem: social enterprises of various kinds (social cooperatives, enterprises engaged in the employment of specific groups, enterprises offering services to the poor, etc.) and social enterprises that are not yet fully operational, public actors (Ministry of Employment, Ministry of Health and Social Affairs, Ministry of Reunification, government agency for the promotion of social enterprise), actors from the world of cooperatives (cooperative research center, Hansalim research center, federation of medical cooperatives), actors involved in the financing of social enterprises (Social Solidarity Bank, Korea Social Investment, Ashoka Korea, Beautiful Foundation, Dasomi Foundation, Merry Year Social Company), local authorities that have developed support mechanisms for social enterprises (Seoul City Social Economy Center, Wonju and Chuncheon City Social Economy Networks), academic actors in research and/or training relating to social enterprises (Sungkonghoe, Hanshin and Ewha Universities in Seoul, Hallym University in Chuncheon, Busan National University, Chonnam National University) and large companies that have developed CSR (corporate social responsibility) policies in conjunction with social enterprises (SK Center for Social Entrepreneurship, Posco Songdo Social Enterprise).

The interviews we conducted with them, spread over several visits and several years, did not follow a constant pattern and were oriented differently according to the type of interlocutor. For the social enterprises questioned or studied, we drew on the main objectives for follow-ups and questions raised in the framework of the ICSEM project of international comparison of social enterprise models[2]. This allowed us to gather information on the genesis of the structures interviewed, their social mission and their target audiences; identify the modalities of their governance and decision-making; obtain information on their financing structure; and understand the main issues they faced. When they were conducted with organizations in the ecosystem, such as the public actors concerned or the foundations providing financial support to social enterprises, these interviews allowed us to gather information on the administrative processes of support to social enterprises, the main strategic orientations, the public resources mobilized and the priorities accorded in the programs.

Our research is therefore based on the constitution and analysis of an essentially qualitative material collected through bibliographic research, interviews and field visits. The social enterprise being an emerging concept, we felt it was essential, indeed inevitable, to identify the concepts and the conditions of stabilization by relying on qualitative data insofar as quantitative data are still rare and often unsystematic and very incomplete. When they exist, they nevertheless allow us to appreciate the order of magnitude of the phenomenon studied and its evolution.

4.3. A typology of the main forms of social enterprises observed in South Korea

The analysis of the information gathered shows that the law of promotion of the social enterprise introduced in 2006 and supported by the Ministry of Labor is one of the main structuring elements of the Korean social enterprise ecosystem. This law introduces an official approval for initiatives that are related to the issue of integrating the unemployed and/or providing social services to disadvantaged groups and specifies the characteristics required for an enterprise to be approved. By the end of 2019, approximately 2,350

---

2 For more information on this project, see: https://emes.net/research-projects/social-enterprise/icsem-project-home/icsem-project-research-partners/ (accessed March 28, 2023).

companies had obtained this approval; they employed just under 50,000 people.

However, our analysis also shows that the 2006 law is not sufficient to account for the reality and complexity of social enterprise in Korea because it does not capture the diversity of concrete forms that this concept covers, nor does it make it possible to define a homogeneous category, since it acts as a label and aggregates forms of organization with very different legal statuses. The reality of social enterprise in Korea is complicated by the fact that there were already measures in place prior to the 2006 law that were aimed at initiatives that were similar to social enterprise, but which did not necessarily fall within the scope of the 2006 law once it had been passed, and by the fact that the 2006 law led to the implementation of complementary public measures, The 2006 law has also led to the creation of complementary national and local public schemes to encourage the development of initiatives in specific areas that have more or less the same characteristics as social enterprises or initiatives that are more likely to receive certification in the future. In other words, there are now certified social enterprises (2006 law), enterprises in the process of certification and enterprises that are not certified but meet the main criteria of a social enterprise.

Through a number of recently introduced public measures, several ministries closely accompany and structure these different forms of social enterprise: the 2006 law for the promotion of social enterprise is carried by the Ministry of Labor, the support scheme for "community enterprises" is coordinated by the Ministry of the Interior, the scheme for "rural community enterprises" is the responsibility of the Ministry of Agriculture (these schemes are discussed in more detail below in our typology of forms of social enterprise), the 2000 law on minimum income, carried by the Ministry of Health and Social Affairs, aims to guide beneficiaries towards the creation of enterprises inspired by the workers' cooperative model (Hwang 2004; Noh et al. 2010) and the 2012 Cooperative Framework Act (Cooperatives) carried by the Ministry of Strategy and Finance regulates the establishment of social and worker cooperatives (Jang 2013). In the space of about 15 years, a relatively complex administrative and legal ecosystem has finally been built in South Korea around the concept of social enterprise (Eum and Bidet 2014; UNRISD 2018).

From the information and knowledge gathered, we have drawn up an initial typology of the forms of social enterprise according to their institutionalization trajectory, their social purpose and their relationship with public mechanisms, whether aimed or not at social enterprise (as mentioned earlier, these criteria are closely linked to the objectives of the ICSEM project; other criteria could generate a different typology). This led us to distinguish three main categories of social enterprises and then to distinguish within these three categories several specific forms of social enterprises according to their purpose(s), target audience and operating mode. In this way, we identified eight main forms of social enterprise in three groups (Table 4.1): (1) forms of social enterprise resulting from public policies explicitly aimed at social enterprise (after the 2006 law mentioned above, specific measures were introduced by several ministries to encourage the creation of social enterprises); (2) forms of social enterprise resulting from the reinterpretation of existing experiences (existing initiatives were reinterpreted and transformed in the light of interest in the social enterprise model); and (3) forms of social enterprise that are emerging and have not yet been institutionalized.

Categories	Forms of social enterprise	Types
(1) Forms of social enterprise resulting from public policies explicitly aimed at social enterprises	Initiatives for employment for seniors	1
	Community businesses	2
	Rural community enterprises	3
(2) Forms of social enterprise arising from the reinterpretation of existing experiences	Social enterprises targeting people with disabilities	4
	Medical cooperatives	5
	Entrepreneurial initiatives targeting marginalized groups (victims of prostitution, North Korean refugees, immigrants, etc.)	6
(3) Emerging social enterprise forms not yet institutionalized	Social ventures for youth	7
	Entrepreneurial initiatives for a more ethical society	8

Table 4.1. *Main forms of social enterprises in Korea*

Employment initiatives for seniors are aimed at older people (65 years or older) in a country where the issue of population aging became crucial in the mid-2000s. One of its dimensions concerns the employment of the elderly, as Korea is characterized by a particularly high employment rate for senior citizens in a context where the pension system is not very generous and still benefits a minority. This is reflected in an official poverty rate of close to 50% for the over-65s. Support for companies employing senior citizens as a majority was quickly identified as one of the answers to this question, but there are no statistics available to assess the scale of these structures. However, it should be noted that they have appeared in areas as varied as small-scale industry, personal services and delivery services and small-scale trade. The salaries paid to older workers are generally quite low, and these initiatives are often led by social workers working in the various structures for the elderly.

Community enterprises are part of a specific scheme introduced in 2010 by the Ministry of Security and Public Administration to promote the development of structures linked to territorial projects. To be certified as such, a community enterprise must have at least five local residents as partners who must own at least 10% of the capital. In most cases, these initiatives involve local grassroots organizations and local authorities. The scheme, which has benefited around 1,500 companies to date, draws on both grassroots initiatives to promote local development projects and public employment programs introduced at the time of the 2008 economic crisis. The aim is to encourage entrepreneurial projects that mobilize essentially local resources to meet the needs or create jobs in a given area. The activities developed are very varied, ranging from the manufacture of products from local resources or traditional techniques to the revitalization of local markets, including activities related to the environment (e.g. recycling), renewable energies, education and trade.

The rural community enterprise in rural areas form was inspired by the experiences of young urban residents who brought environmental issues to rural areas. These experiences then inspired a specific positive communication introduced in 2010 by the Ministry of Agriculture to encourage the development of initiatives that are more broadly focused on meeting the specific needs of rural communities. About 1000 enterprises are or have been supported through this scheme, which defines a community enterprise in a rural area as "an enterprise based on voluntary participation and the mobilization of local resources that contributes to local development by creating jobs and generating resources for the community". The positive scheme categorizes these initiatives in five ways according to their main purpose: (1) processing agricultural products; (2) promoting exchanges between rural and urban areas (e.g. through agri-tourism); (3) providing social services to local residents; (4) consulting for local development; and (5) hybrids of several of these purposes. In nearly 60% of these structures, the term "community" is used in reference to the notion of the village and the condition is to involve more than half of the village's inhabitants. It should be noted, however, that 80% of the jobs generated are precarious and that these initiatives are not very sustainable, particularly because they have difficulty building partnerships with traditional cooperative actors in rural areas (agricultural and fishing cooperatives).

Social enterprises targeting people with disabilities are part of a broader public policy for the employment of people with disabilities that has been developed in Korea since the early 1980s involving various ministries and civil society actors. We have distinguished in this category two forms of social enterprise presenting distinct characteristics: professional rehabilitation structures, which are non-profit organizations depending on the Ministry of Social Affairs, and standard workshops, which are private companies certified by the Ministry of Labour. Both respond to specific constraints relating to the employment of disabled people, but they also employ social workers whose salaries are largely financed by public funds. Vocational rehabilitation structures (around 380 for just over 10,000 jobs) are not very autonomous organizations that depend on a parent structure of the social vocation foundation type. The standard workshops (around 50 for about 1,800 jobs) are more conventional businesses that derive most of their resources from the sale of goods and services.

Medical cooperatives emerged in the mid-1990s to provide health services to local populations with inadequate access to medical care. Initially targeting disadvantaged groups (farmers, immigrants, working poor, etc.), they have also attracted users seeking a more ethical and participatory approach to health. They first used the legal status of consumer cooperatives introduced in Korea in 1998 and then transformed into social cooperatives as defined by the 2012 Cooperative Framework Law (Eum and Bidet 2014). These are non-profit structures that employ healthcare professionals (doctors, nurses), social workers and administrative staff. The medical cooperative can be considered a form of social enterprise offering highly professionalized services within a framework of democratic governance framed by cooperative principles. It represents, from this point of view, a form of social enterprise that has proven to be particularly sustainable and that has been able to acquire a size that is quite significant, while at the same time being part of a vision of a more inclusive, more responsible and more frugal healthcare system.

Entrepreneurial initiatives aimed at marginalized groups regroup different kinds of structures according to their target audience: the homeless, victims of prostitution, North Korean migrants, etc. These three categories have their own public support schemes, but they can also be supported under social enterprise schemes, as the specific groups they target are identified as a potential beneficiary group in the 2006 law promoting social enterprises. Some public schemes, such as those dependent on the Ministry of Reunification, also target structures to "pre-certify" them for social enterprise approval from the Ministry of Labour. In most cases, it is a question of providing employment to persons falling within the category concerned in activities which may be very varied but are in general low-skilled (catering, cleaning, retail trade, packaging, etc.). Statistical data on these forms of social enterprises are very imperfect. The pre-certification program of the Ministry of Reunification, for example, lists some 50 structures geared towards the employment of North Korean migrants.

Social enterprises for youth emerged from a program launched in 2011 by the state-owned Korea Social Enterprise Promotion Agency. This program provides support for one year to social entrepreneurship initiatives by young people under 25 years of age. Although they are set up and managed voluntarily by self-nominated groups, these initiatives are in line with objectives defined by the public authorities and are accompanied by consultants selected by the government. Their autonomy is therefore relative and their sustainability is very uncertain once the public support ends because few of them generate sufficient profits, which does not allow them to employ staff. Legally, they often remain informal structures during the first year and then disappear or become legally structured if they have acquired sufficiently solid foundations to hope to be sustainable. They embody a form of social enterprise that is still not very institutionalized and whose specific characteristics distinguish it from the other forms identified.

They have developed activities related to education, social services, the environment, management of green spaces, personal services, sports, culture, tourism, etc.

Entrepreneurial initiatives for a more ethical society refer to initiatives whose stated objective is to contribute to promoting an alternative model based on social, ethical or ecological values. Since they are not part of any public system, they can take a wide variety of legal forms and, for the most part, enjoy a high degree of autonomy. These initiatives belong mainly to two movements: on the one hand, an alternative movement that advocates collective approaches around activities such as cafés, libraries, popular education programs or cultural activities; on the other hand, an entrepreneurial movement, often led by individual entrepreneurs, who develop their activity independently of both public mechanisms and large companies. These are often inspired and supported by foundations promoting social entrepreneurship, such as the Ashoka Foundation or the Beautiful Foundation, within the framework of support programs for projects in the fields of the environment, human rights, education, culture, etc.

4.4. Discussion: Understanding Korean social enterprise in the light of the EMES ideal type

To better understand what distinguishes these different forms of social enterprises in their functioning, we have chosen to compare them to the EMES ideal of a social enterprise. The EMES ideal type was developed from research conducted in the 1990s in a dozen European countries (Defourny and Nyssens 2013). It identifies nine criteria characteristic of social enterprises, grouped in a first version into two dimensions (economic and social) before being subsequently arranged in three dimensions (economic, social and participatory governance) to better highlight the democratic governance specific to social enterprises in Europe. Martinet and Payaud (2007), in particular, have used this approach to produce a taxonomy of CSR strategies. This approach seems to us to be interesting for two reasons: on the one hand, it allows us to identify the aspects that differentiate the forms of social enterprise observed in Korea, and on the other hand, it allows us to better understand how the European approach to social enterprise, which was used to construct the EMES ideal type, differs from the Korean vision.

In this research, for each of the criteria associated with the three dimensions of the EMES model, we assigned a score from 1 to 5 depending on whether the elements at our disposal led us to consider that the form of social enterprise studied did not fulfill this criterion or fulfilled it pefectly. The highest score (5) was given when compliance with the criterion in question was guaranteed by the legal status itself. For example, the legal framework of the social cooperative, which is used in particular by medical cooperatives, offers the guarantee that the organization that uses it has a democratic governance and does not distribute its profits to its members. In the absence of precise statutory rules corresponding to the EMES criterion under consideration, we mobilized the information accumulated from the observation of existing structures (information from interviews, official documents such as activity and financial reports, elements provided by existing academic works) and assigned a score of 4 when we found that this information showed that the practice was generally consistent with the EMES criterion, a score of 3 when it showed that the practice was diverse and a score of 2 when it showed that the practice was generally far from the EMES criterion. A score of 1 was reserved for organizations whose legal status did not coincide with the EMES criterion at all. This method allowed us to obtain a score for each form of social enterprise identified (Table 4.2). According to our method, a score of 45 thus represents an identification with the EMES ideal type of social enterprise.

First of all, we note that the scores obtained by each of the eight forms of social enterprise considered varied from 26 to 44, but the majority of the forms surveyed obtain a score between 30 and 39. However, our study revealed two extreme cases (Table 4.2): on the one hand, the medical cooperative (form five), which almost perfectly matched the EMES ideal type (score of 44), and on the other hand, social enterprises for young people (form seven), which were very far from it (score of 26).

The close proximity between the medical cooperative and the EMES ideal is logical insofar as the latter was strongly inspired by the cooperative model, which is particularly important in Europe, and more specifically that of the social cooperative that appeared in Italy and which is also the legal status that Korean medical cooperatives have been using since the introduction of the General Cooperative Act of 2012. According to this law, a social cooperative is defined by specific conditions regarding surplus distribution (non-profit), governance (multi-partnership) and the pursuit of a social utility defined in reference to a territory or to a specific category of beneficiaries.

Ideal EMES Type	Form One	Form Two	Form Three	Form Four	Form Five	Form Six	Form Seven	Form Eight
Economic dimension								
(1) Continuous production activity	4	4	4	4	5	5	2	4
(2) Paid employment	3	4	4	4	5	5	2	4
(3) Level of economic risk	3	5	4	5	5	4	2	4
Social dimension								
(4) Social objective	5	5	5	4	4	5	4	3
(5) Limited distribution of profit	3	3	4	3	5	4	3	3
(6) Autonomous initiative	4	3	4	2	5	4	3	4
Dimension of democratic governance								
(7) Degree of autonomy	3	3	3	4	5	4	2	5
(8) Participatory governance	3	4	3	2	5	3	3	3
(9) Decision-making process	5	3	3	3	5	3	5	5
Overall score	33	34	34	31	44	37	26	35

Table 4.2. *Forms of social enterprises and criteria of the EMES ideal type*

However, the social enterprise for young people embodies the form of social enterprise furthest removed from the EMES-type ideal. These are usually experimental initiatives, not formalized legally and closely controlled by the public agencies that support them in the initial phase. Their profitability is often low and very fragile, and the most sustainable ones can adopt any entrepreneurial form (non-profit enterprise, cooperative, capital enterprise, etc.). In reference to the EMES ideal, these are therefore structures whose economic dimension is still very fragile due to a lack of maturity, whose status is often informal and which are essentially exploratory and not very autonomous with respect to the public actors who support them.

After medical cooperatives, initiatives targeting very specific groups (homeless people, victims of prostitution, North Korean migrants) scored the highest (37). Like medical cooperatives, this is also a social enterprise (form six) that falls into the second category in our initial typology, the one that brings together forms of social enterprise prior to the establishment of public schemes targeting social enterprises. Due to their social purpose, these initiatives have in fact quite easily integrated one or another of the mechanisms targeting social enterprises, without systematically going towards the one proposed by the 2006 law.

It is interesting to note the differences that separate the different forms of social enterprises aimed at specific audiences according to the audiences targeted: the overall scores obtained by each of the three main forms of social enterprises brought together in this set varied from 31 (form four: social enterprises targeting people with disabilities) to 37 (form seven: entrepreneurial initiatives aimed at marginalized groups) via 33 (form one: initiatives for the employment of seniors). Each of these three forms of social enterprise has its own characteristics, but they have in common a significant distance from the ideal type for the dimension of democratic governance.

The two forms of social enterprises based on the community enterprise model (forms two and three), i.e. on a territorial basis, also offer an interesting comparison with an identical overall score (34), but have some specific characteristics, in particular a greater proximity with the social dimension of the EMES ideal type for the community enterprises in rural areas. There remains one last form of social enterprise: entrepreneurial initiatives for a more ethical society (form eight), which obtained an intermediate score (35) with good proximity for the economic and democratic governance dimensions, but a greater distance for the social dimension, reflecting in particular a more global social purpose, a positioning on the fringes of public systems and a more pronounced anchoring in individual entrepreneurship.

Beyond the overall score obtained, considering each dimension of the EMES model separately allows us to refine our observation and understanding of the characteristics specific to each form of social enterprise considered. This provides additional insights into the perception and complexity of what social enterprise is in Korea. Assuming that a score of 10 or less (out of a possible 15) reflects a significant distance from the ideal type, we can first point out that only one form of social enterprise accumulates a great distance for all three dimensions (social enterprises for young people) and only one other form accumulates a great distance with two of the three dimensions (social enterprises targeting people with disabilities). For all the other forms surveyed, the score was below 10 for only one dimension or, most often, above 10 for all three dimensions. If we now compare the scores obtained for each dimension of the EMES model, the social dimension has the highest scores, while the democratic governance dimension has the lowest.

4.5. Conclusion

We used the EMES ideal type constructed from the observation of social enterprises in Europe to better define the characteristics of the different forms of social enterprises that we identified in Korea. The results finally led us to consider a classification slightly different from the one initially carried out on the basis of the institutional trajectory and the stated purpose. Three groups emerged according to their proximity to the EMES ideal type: a group that corresponded closely to the ideal type (score above 10 for each dimension), where we found the medical cooperatives and initiatives in favor of marginalized groups; a majority group that corresponded well to two of the three dimensions of the ideal type; and a group that was further from the ideal type (score below 10 for two or three of the dimensions), in which were placed the social enterprises for youth and the social enterprises targeting people with disabilities.

The great diversity of social enterprises observed in South Korea makes it difficult to believe that there is a unified model of social enterprise that is specific to or dominant in each national context, as authors such as Kerlin (2013) have suggested. Rather, it reinforces the idea, formalized by Defourny and Nyssens (2017a, 2017b), that several major models of social enterprise coexist in each national context, which are changing and in tension. In the Korean context, the existing forms of social enterprise are the result of diverse trajectories and tensions reflecting bottom-up and top-down approaches, neither of which is completely driven by the same motives or values. We can see the influences of models that have appeared elsewhere, such as those of British community business, Italian social cooperatives or social entrepreneurship.

However, our study indicates that the vast majority of the concrete forms of social enterprises identified in Korea have one feature in common: they are quite far from a model of enterprise with democratic governance or participatory governance. This may be seen as an indicator of the influence of the North American conception of social enterprise, in which this element is not valued, but it is also, in our view, a reflection of a cultural particularity specific to Korea and probably to a part of Confucian Asia, where the values of hierarchy, respect for authority and inequality are frequently emphasized to the detriment of the principle of equality between individuals on which democratic governance is based. The cultural specificity of the Korean context, which has long been marked by a pronounced cultural and political embedding of civil society (Bidet 2002), explains why democratic governance is a notion that is not easy to implement in the economic field and why, on the contrary, the influence of highly hierarchical structures and public supervision is particularly strong there and constitutes a structuring element that is essential, including for the social enterprise. However, the dynamics of the social enterprise phenomenon show that Korean society is gradually breaking free from this political and cultural straitjacket.

Our study also points out that many forms of social enterprise derive a significant part of their resources from public schemes that provide them with essential resources, whether financial (subsidies), tax (exemptions) or in the form of support and training. Kim and Moon (2017) have shown that financial support from the public authorities was one of the main instruments for the emergence and growth of social enterprises in Korea and that the central challenge for many was to establish a viable operating model during this three- to five-year support period. In contrast to the previous findings, this aspect reflects an orientation of the social enterprise closer to the European model than to the American model, which focuses primarily on market resources. On the contrary, public resources seem to be essential to the emergence of Korean social enterprises, which are developed in the framework of a multi-year public/private partnership in which the social enterprise model appears as a "political entrepreneur" (Lee 2015) that inspires new public measures at the same time as it becomes one of the tools for implementing public policies in terms of job creation, social inclusion of disadvantaged groups, community development and the production of social or medical services for which existing actors do not provide a sufficient or sufficiently diversified response.

One of the main challenges facing social enterprises in Korea is to find a balance that allows them to survive and develop in the context of a gradual withdrawal of the various forms of public support. The answer to this challenge undoubtedly lies in the implementation of stricter control of the structures supported in order to avoid windfall effects and free riders who come to take advantage of a public subsidy without any real concern for sustainability and in increased professionalization of the activities of these structures and the professions that result from them.

4.6. References

Alter, K. (2007). *Social Enterprise Typology*. Virtue Ventures LLC, Wilmington [Online]. Available at: http://www.4lenses.org/setypology.

Bayle, E. and Dupuis, J.C. (eds) (2012). *Management des entreprises de l'économie sociale et solidaire*. De Boeck, Brussels.

Bidet, E. (2002). Explaining the third-sector in South Korea. *Voluntas*, 13(2), 131–147.

Bidet, E. and Defourny, J. (eds) (2019). *Social Enterprise in Asia: Theory, Models and Practice*. Routledge, New York.

Borzaga, C. and Defourny, J. (eds) (2001). *The Emergence of Social Enterprise*. Routledge, New York.

Boutillier, S. (2009). Aux origines de l'entrepreneuriat social. Les affaires selon Jean-Baptiste André Godin (1817–1888). *Innovations*, 30, 115–134.

Chaves, R. and Monzon, J.L. (2012). *The Social Economy in the European Union*. European Economic and Social Committee, Brussels.

Dart, R. (2004). The legitimacy of social enterprise. *Nonprofit Management and Leadership*, 14(4), 411–424.

Dees, J.G. (1996). Social enterprise spectrum: Philanthropy to commerce. *Harvard Business Review*, 9, 396–343.

Defourny, J. and Nyssens, M. (2010). Conceptions of social enterprise and social entrepreneurship in Europe and the United States: Convergences and differences. *Journal of Social Entrepreneurship*, 1(1), 32–53.

Defourny, J. and Nyssens, M. (2013). L'approche EMES de l'entreprise sociale dans une perspective comparative. SOCENT working paper 2013/01.

Defourny, J. and Nyssens, M. (eds) (2017a). *Économie sociale et solidaire*. De Boeck, Brussels.

Defourny, J. and Nyssens, M. (2017b). Fundamentals for an international typology of social enterprise models. *Voluntas*, 28(6), 2469–2497.

Desroche, H. (1976). *Le Projet coopératif*. Éditions ouvrières, Paris.

Drucker, P. (1990). *Managing the Nonprofit Organization*. Butterworth-Heinemann, Oxford.

Duverger, T. (2016). *L'économie sociale et solidaire : une histoire de la société civile en France et en Europe de 1968 à nos jours*. Le Bord de l'eau, Lormont.

Eum, H. and Bidet, E. (2014). Dynamiques de l'économie sociale en Corée du Sud. *Revue internationale de l'économie sociale*, 332, 30–45.

Ferraton, C. (2007). *Associations et coopératives. Une autre histoire économique*. Érès, Paris.

Gaiger, I., Nyssens, M., Wanderley, F. (eds) (2019). *Social Enterprise in Latin America: Theory, Models and Practice*. Routledge, New York.

Gueslin, A. (1998). *L'invention de l'économie sociale*. Economica, Paris.

Hansmann, H. (1980). The role of nonprofit enterprise. *Faculty Scholarship Series*, 5048 [Online]. Available at: https://digitalcommons.law.yale.edu/fss_papers/5048.

Hwang, D.S. (2004). Job creation through social enterprise and social jobs. *International Labor Brief*, 2(5), 1–3.

James, E. and Rose-Acherman, S. (1986). *The Nonprofit Enterprise in Market Economics*. Harwood Academic Publishers, Reading.

Jang, J. (2013). Republic of Korea. In *International Handbook of Cooperative Law*, Cragogna, D., Fici, A., Henry, H. (eds). Springer, Berlin.

Kerlin, J.A. (2013). Defining social enterprise across different contexts: A conceptual framework based on institutional factors. *Nonprofit and Voluntary Sector Quarterly*, 42(1), 84–108.

Kim, T.H. and Moon, M.J. (2017). Using social enterprises for social policy in South Korea: Do funding and management affect social and economic performance? *Public Administration and Development*, 37(1), 15–27.

Lee, E. (2015). Social enterprise, policy entrepreneurs, and the third sector: The case of South Korea. *Voluntas*, 26, 1084–1099.

Light, P. (2008). *The Search For Social Entrepreneurship*. The Brookings Institution, Washington.

Martinet, A.C. and Payaud, M. (2007). Formes de RSE et entreprises sociales : une hybridation des stratégies. *Revue française de gestion*, 11, 199–214.

Nicholls, A. (ed.) (2006). *Social Entrepreneurship. New Models of Sustainable Social Change*. Oxford University Press, Oxford.

Noh, D.M., Kim, S.Y., Jang, W.B., Kim, M.K. (2010). A study on the public supports for the third sector in Korea. Working paper, Korea Institute for Health and Social Affairs, Chungcheong.

Nyssens, M. (2006). *The Social Enterprise at the Crossroads of Market, Public Policies and Civil Society*. Routledge, New York.

Powell, W. and Steinberg, D. (1987). *The Nonprofit Sector: A Research Handbook*. Yale University Press, London.

Salamon, L. and Anheier, H. (1996). *The Emerging Nonprofit Sector*. Manchester University Press, New York.

Shin, M.H. (2009). Essay for construction of social economy concept in Korea. *Tendency and Perspective*, 75, 11–36.

Spear, R. and Bidet, E. (2005). Social enterprise for work integration in 12 European countries: A descriptive analysis. *Annals of Public and Cooperative Economics*, 76(2), 195–231.

UNRISD (2018). Social and solidarity economy for the Sustainable Development Goals. Spotlight on the social economy in Seoul. Report, United Nations Research Institute for Social Development, Geneva.

Vienney, C. (1981). Socio-économie des organisations coopératives. Report, Coopérative d'Information et d'Édition Mutualiste, Paris.

Weisbrod, B. (1978). *The Voluntary Nonprofit Sector: An Economic Analysis*. Lexington Books, Pennsylvania.

Weisbrod, B. (1988). *The Nonprofit Economy*. Harvard University Press, Cambridge.

Young, D. (1983). *If Not for Profit, for What?* Lexington Books, Pennsylvania.

Young, D. (2007). A unified theory of social enterprise. Working paper 07–01, Nonprofit Studies program, Andrew Young School of Policy Studies, Atlanta.

PART 2

Social Innovations by Inclusive Companies Within a Territory

5

Managing Inclusion and Diversity in Organizations: A Strategic Approach to Human Capital

It is critical, at this point, that executives, managers and team leaders know how to build and institutionalize an inclusive organizational culture. They must comprehend how to exercise inclusive leadership, decrease and eliminate bias to maximize employee engagement and participative management and use cross-cultural communication skills to enhance organizational innovation and productivity.

5.1. An overview of the most current literature

According to Bauer, Erdogan, Caughlin and Truxillo (2018), diversity refers to real or perceived differences among individuals concerning race, color, creed, national origin, age, physical and/or mental ability, and religion and the concomitant attributes that may affect their interrelationships with other coworkers, and creating an organizational culture of inclusion is very beneficial to a business. They assert that the potential of diversity is unlocked when diversity is fully accompanied by inclusion. They define an inclusive working environment as an organization in which individuals of all backgrounds "are treated with dignity and respect, are included in

Chapter written by Douglas McCabe. The author wishes to thank Elisabeth Di Biagio for her help with the bibliographic research.

decision-making, and are valued for who they are and what they bring to the group or organization". Additionally, inclusiveness allows individuals to be themselves. Everyone is valued not only for their performance but also as human beings. Employees have input in decision-making, and everyone's ideas are heard. In this author's opinion, this is an excellent definition. These four scholars also state that evidence-based research demonstrates that, when accompanied by the principle of inclusion, diversity has positive and proactive effects on workgroups and teams in the form of lower interpersonal and unit conflict. Furthermore, "perceptions of equal access to opportunities and fair treatment are associated with positive outcomes for individuals". Indeed, this is a paramount organizational justice issue in the employment relationship. Finally, they maintain that an inclusive work environment is critically important for innovation. They state the following: "When people with different life experiences and viewpoints come together and share information, disclose their perspectives, and make an effort to integrate them, they arrive at more innovative decisions."

Gowan and Lepak (2020) emphasize that training is essential for leading inclusiveness in terms of managing employees for competitive advantage. They state that inclusion training aids in reducing discrimination by making coworkers more aware of the discrimination that occurs both overtly and covertly in the employment and enhances understanding of the importance and value of having an open and welcoming workplace for all employees. Additionally, they mention benchmarks for effective inclusiveness training, such as incorporating training into a bigger and more extensive set of diversity initiatives, spreading the training over a larger period of time rather than it happening all at once, having participants set specific goals related to inclusion in the workplace and targeting training to awareness skills.

5.1.1. *Ethical issues*

Another set of scholars, Jones and George (2019), emphasize the topic's strategic and ethical aspects. According to them, inclusion and diversity raise crucial ethical and social responsibility issues. First, they point out that there is an ethical imperative that diverse individuals must receive equal opportunities in organizations and must be treated fairly and justly. Second, there is substantial evidence-based research that individuals of different races, colors and creeds continue to experience unfair and disparate treatment in corporations and companies due to biases, stereotypes and even overt discrimination.

Furthermore, Jones and George (2019) explore some particular ethical issues. Managers and team leaders must be vigilant to ensure that employees are not discriminated against because of their age. It is an ethical issue that executives and managers need to ensure that the organizational procedures and policies they have in place treat all employees fairly and justly, regardless of their age. Moreover, the increasing racial and ethnic diversity of the workplace as an entirety underscores the strategic importance of effectively managing inclusion. Continuing their ethics theme, another vital issue for managers is recognizing religious diversity and being sensitive to different religions and their belief systems. Specifically, critical business meetings should not be scheduled during a holy day for members of a particular faith. Team leaders should exercise flexibility in allowing their employees to have time off for religious observances.

Jones and George (2019) discuss three other ethical issues: disabilities, socio-economic background and sexual orientation. Regarding the accommodation for disabilities issue, they believe that a challenge for companies is to promote a work environment in which employees who need accommodation feel comfortable disclosing their need for it while concomitantly ensuring that the accommodations not only enable those with disabilities to perform their jobs effectively "but also are perceived to be fair by those who are not disabled". Regarding the socio-economic background, from a management perspective, these management scholars assert that socio-economic diversity requires that front-line managers be sensitive and responsive to the family concerns of individuals who might not be as well off as others. Finally, they pronounce that all organizations must recognize the minority status of LGBTQ employees and "affirm their rights to fair and equal treatment".

Finally, Jones and George (2019) bring up some other types of diversity issues that are critical for team leaders to effectively deal with inclusion efforts – in this case, physical appearance. From an ethical perspective, managers need to make sure that all workplace individuals are treated fairly, justly and equitably regardless of their physical appearance. In summary, managers have an ethical obligation from an ethical/business perspective to prevent employee treatment disparities.

5.1.2. *International cross-cultural inclusion*

In contrast, Du Brin (2016) emphasizes issues relating to cultural diversity and the need to institutionalize training programs to aid employees in value diversity and improve cross-cultural relationships, particularly in overseas relationships. The emphasis in these programs should be to strengthen the relationships between people of different cultural and demographic groups. Cultural training aims to help employees understand individuals from other cultures. These programs can improve workplace relationships.

Du Brin (2016) posits several implications for managerial practice on this topic. First, he states that it is essential as a practicing manager to keep promoting the idea that diversity is meant to be inclusive. Second, employers must develop a global mindset, a feeling of confidence and comfort with workers from different countries. Third, and finally, he believes that the true meaning of valuing diversity is to respect a wide range of cultural and individual differences.

5.1.3. *Barriers to inclusion and diversity*

Kinicki and Williams (2020) lay out powerful delineation barriers to inclusion and diversity. They note that resistance to change is a common attitude that slaps managers in the face all the time. These barriers must be overcome to have an inclusive work organization.

First of all, there is the issue of stereotypes and prejudices. According to these two scholars, when employees view differences as weaknesses, many employees may express this as a potential concern, and diversity hiring will lead to sacrifice in terms of competence. Second, there may be a fear of discrimination against the majority of group members – i.e. a group of employees may be fearful that attempts to achieve a higher level of inclusion in their departments will automatically result in bias against the majority group. Third, there may be resistance to the priorities of the inclusion program priorities. What is meant by this? It means that some employees may be resentful that the diversity/inclusion-promoting organizational policies will be reimbursed in the firm's performance appraisal and merit-pay reward systems. Fourth, and finally, when there is the existence of an overall negative diversity climate, which would be a sub-component of the organization's overall culture, this could be a barrier.

To summarize at this point from this author's perspective, it is clear that practicing the principle of having an inclusive organizational philosophy is an excellent opportunity to use and develop all of the human resources within an organization for the symbolic benefit of both the organization and the employees. One of the key benefits of inclusion's diversity is a plethora and multiplicity of perspectives and ideas available to the firm. For example, a diverse workforce can provide a corporation with greater knowledge of consumer preferences in the marketplace. Additionally, an inclusive organization can give a firm a much better competitive edge in the truly international economy by facilitating a better understanding and comprehension of other customs vis-à-vis new needs in the marketplace.

5.1.4. *Reinforcing inclusive behavior*

Managing inclusion means not only accommodating employees' differences but supporting and using the differences to the company's advantage. According to Bateman and Snell (2009), today's firms are approaching inclusion and diversity from a strategic business-oriented perspective. Increasingly, inclusion can be a powerful tool for building a competitive advantage over competitors. For example, corporations with a solid reputation for providing an inclusive working environment should have a competitive advantage in the local, regional or national labor market because the most highly qualified employees will seek out these firms. Furthermore, when workers perceive that their differences are truly valued, they will, in all likelihood, become more productive, committed and loyal organizational citizens.

Bateman and Snell (2009) note that there may be principles to secure an inclusive organization. First, securing top management leadership and commitment is essential for inclusion efforts and programs to succeed. Unless this first step is taken, the rest of the company will not take the effort seriously. According to them, this could be accomplished by incorporating the company's perspectives towards inclusion into its mission statement and by top management participating on a mandatory basis in diversity programs.

Second, they assert that the next step in reinforcing inclusion is to establish an ongoing and continuous assessment of the company's practices and organizational policies in the critical arenas of recruitment measures and promotions. The key objective here is to identify problem areas and make substantive recommendations where organizational changes are needed. Third, firms should attract a diverse workforce by accommodating employees' family and work needs in offering alternative work arrangements. Fourth, managers and team leaders need to build awareness of the importance of inclusion. They need to sensitize their workers to the various assumptions they make about others in the ways those various assumptions affect their decision-making judgments. Fifth, and finally, it is often useful to remember that diversity measures are also there to ensure that deserving employees have a chance to progress in the hierarchy.

Thus, as we can discern, diversity means all of the ways in which individuals differ. Anything that makes each individual unique is part of the denotation of diversity. Furthermore, inclusion encourages executives, managers and team leaders to put the concepts and practices of diversity into concrete action by laying the groundwork of creating an organizational environment of total respect and involvement where diverse ideas and backgrounds and a multiplicity of perspectives can be harnessed to create a better company.

The research by Sherbin and Rashlil (2017) indicates that inclusive leadership is an amalgamation of six major behaviors: (a) ensuring that employees speak up and are thoroughly and adequately heard; (b) making it safe for all team members to propose new and novel ideas; (c) empowering employees to make decisions where appropriate; (d) giving actionable and timely feedback; (e) sharing credit with all the team members for team success; and (f) taking advice. They conclude the research by strongly asserting that diversity without inclusion is sad because it causes mixed opportunities. On the other hand, diversity coupled with inclusion produces a powerful mix of talent utilization and engagement.

As we begin to conclude this overview of the most current literature on the topics of diversity and inclusion, I would like to discuss the work and research of Bourke and Espedido (2019). Their research focuses on the very specific topic of making executives and managers' actions more inclusive. Their large-scale survey research indicated six traits or behaviors that distinguish inclusive leaders from others in leadership positions. First, inclusive leaders articulate a truly authentic commitment to the principle of diversity, hold other managers accountable and make inclusion a personal priority in their companies. Second, they practice managerial humility and create opportunities for employees to contribute. Third, they are aware of bias in their organization systems. Fourth, inclusive managers possess an open mindset and empathize with their subordinates. Fifth, they are very attentive to cross-cultural differences. Sixth, and finally, they are skilled in effective collaboration. They conclude that the executives who continuously engage in inclusive leadership will see the results in their very diverse work teams' superior performance in their corporations.

5.2. From research to practice

As we have seen from a systematic review of the literature, an inclusive employer appreciates and gives value to differences in an individual and encourages all employees to be accepting, tolerant and respectful of each coworker. Companies and organizations need to view inclusion and organizational fairness, justice and equity as an integral part of their overall strategic plan. One organization that I am familiar with has just completed that exercise.

According to Ricco and Guerci (2014), employees' differences and the management of diversity engagement need to be introduced and truly and fully integrated into the overall corporate strategy, values and vision. This strategy and vision need to be translated into associative property taxes to promote true organizational changes that affect the entire firm. Thus, employment in diversity and inclusion management should be done in a way that can be adopted to specific organizations. They proposed that firms should adopt an integrated process of change management regarding diversity. This implies treating inclusion efforts as a core, central component of the corporate strategy and introducing them at the tactical and operational levels involving senior management, middle managers, line managers and employees. Finally, they emphasize that diversity and inclusion management should not be confined to mere slogans, ethical codes of conduct and limited training sessions copied from other firms.

In another study (Brimhall 2019), significant direct associations were found between leader engagement, inclusion and innovation. Innovation was linked directly to improved job satisfaction. Significant other effects were found from leader engagement that increased job satisfaction through increased climates for inclusion.

Pasztor (2019) states that research findings reveal three key approaches in how companies frame diversity: first, as a true organizational asset promoted and preserved via its corporate and human resource management values; second, as a legitimate driver of business excellence and competitive advantage; and, third, as an institutional, structural mechanism supported by diversity and inclusion initiatives such as employee networking, mentoring and extensive diversity training.

One particular study in the *Wall Street Journal* (Holger 2019) found that diverse and inclusive cultures provide firms with a competitive advantage over their peers. Many of the companies in the study said that having a well-rounded workforce has helped them create better products and be more innovative, thus leading to growth in sales and profit. As one executive stated in the study: "A diverse team supported by an inclusive environment that values each individual will outperform that homogenous team every time." Another executive in the study emphatically said that: "Our clients are increasingly looking to us for best practices and strategic advice on how to improve their diversity and inclusion efforts."

Another study in the *Wall Street Journal* (Feintzeig 2020) found that to instill lasting change in terms of diversity and inclusion, firms must go beyond the superficial and rethink how they hire, mentor, lead and promote their employees. Companies should not assume that annual diversity training will check the box. As one executive noted: "It's not enough to talk about it if you're not going to actually do it." Additionally, according to the study, real change takes time in the arena of diversity and inclusion. As another manager asserted: "Look internally, find where you and your company have prioritized diversity and where you have fallen short."

Another way to achieve results in the arena of inclusion is to understand our unconscious bias and become aware of it (Pitman 2019). Unconscious bias can have a powerful impact on companies. When it comes to diversity and inclusion, these biases related to race, color, creed, sexual orientation and religion have real implications in the workplace. It is imperative to find and understand the origins of these unconscious biases, address their underlying causes and develop ways to eliminate them.

Jordan (2011) posits the following points regarding achieving results. First, companies must determine what actions they are taking to foster an inclusive work environment where the uniqueness of backgrounds is welcomed and leverage for better business decisions. Next, firms must work from a well-documented plan of action, complete with goals and objectives, to realize organizational change. Finally, they must incorporate diversity principles across the business functions and units and create opportunities for cross-general interactions and work teams.

In an exciting study by Sabharwal (2014), it was found that the need for improving workplace performance as a managerial approach promotes greater inclusion of employees in ways that takes their views into account and promotes their self-esteem. Her study also indicated that improving organizational performance requires leadership that is dedicated to the fostering of inclusion in empowering employees so they can influence work group decisions. Hence, managers' inclusive management style holds greater potential for workplace harmony.

5.3. A case study

In May of 2019, Georgetown University announced the newly formed Office of Student Equity and Inclusion. Although it is a centralized office, Georgetown University is committed to a broad-based, institutionalized approach that makes inclusion and equity a value truly central to its university community. The Office of Student Equity and Inclusion reports to both senior academics and student-affairs leadership, just reflecting on the three-dimensionality of the students' lives. The office has a dual reporting line to the office of the Provost of Georgetown and to the office of the Vice President of Student Affairs. This is a whole-institution approach that engages the entire university community and the work of inclusion. The office wants every dean, senior associate dean, associate dean and assistant dean and every department chair, faculty member and staff member to center on this work. The office believes that there needs to be very explicit conversations about equity, diversity and inclusion. According to the office, success would look like Georgetown University community members having a lucid comprehension that inclusion and equity are priorities that are taken very seriously. Operationally, success would be having more administrators and individuals in positions of leadership and decision-making authority from historically marginalized communities.

It should also be noted that the undergraduate program at Georgetown University's McDonough School of Business has a mission statement on diversity, equity and inclusive excellence. It states the following:

> The Undergraduate Program at Georgetown University's McDonough School of Business, per the University's Mission, embraces inclusive excellence and believes in the importance of fostering an open environment that welcomes all voices of the members of our professional and academic communities. We strive to create physical and intellectual space where students, faculty, and staff of all backgrounds can collaboratively learn, work, and serve together. We are committed to serving as a resource for historically underrepresented populations; to cultivating talent that excels and dynamic, diverse work environments; and to creating positive change for the future. We prepare all business leaders to actively support this mission through collaboration, inquiry, agency and scholarship.

Finally, a new undergraduate course was introduced in the fall of 2020 at Georgetown's McDonough School of Business titled "Global Organizations and Culture: Theory, Methods, And Practice". This seminar allows students to explore their own cultural identities and how their own cultural identity shaped their interactions, expectations and approach to working with others. At the MBA level at the McDonough School of Business at Georgetown, a new course was also introduced in the fall of 2020 titled "Innovation Through Inclusion". The course is designed to help students understand and practice inclusive management skills that will enable them to effectively identify, develop and lead high-impact, data-driven innovations for and with our increasingly diverse world.

5.4. Conclusion

Diversity, coupled with inclusion, can be useful for business (Hunt et al. 2014). Furthermore, there are many measures and techniques that diverse employees already find effective in promoting a more diverse employment relationship with inclusion (Krentz et al. 2019). As has been seen, executives must pay more attention to company culture. An inclusive workplace culture creates more significant organizational equity, fairness and justice. Establishing an employment relationship where each employee feels comfortable will allow them to contribute to the firm. From an institutional perspective, it means executives, managers and team leaders must make sincere efforts so that their employees are aware of and can prevent unconscious bias in the workplace.

What is the final word? Diversity and inclusion efforts will only succeed when integrated into the overall, top-level company strategy by executives.

The topic of inclusion holds a multiplicity of potential arenas of future research. Shore (2011) maintains that much research is still needed to understand how organizations can create inclusive environments that provide opportunities for the variety of individuals who work together in the international, global economy. Farndale (2015) proposes that future research might focus on adopting an employee-level perspective to explain attitudes and perceptions towards different dimensions of diversity and inclusion across country settings. Finally, Samosh (2020) recommends research on the impact of international policy and legislation on individual employee experiences, conceptualizing inclusion at the national level, measuring inclusion at the national level and applying a measurement framework for evaluating the effectiveness of public policy and legislation in relation to inclusion.

5.5. References

Bauer, T., Erdogan, B., Caughlin, D., Truxillo, D (2018). *Human Resource Management: People, Data, and Analytics*. Sage Publications, Thousand Oaks.

Bateman, T.S. and Snell, S.A. (eds) (2009). Managing the diverse workforce. In *Management: Leading and Collaborating in a Competitive World*. McGraw-Hill, New York.

Bleijenbergh, I., Peters, P., Poutsma, E. (2010). Diversity management beyond the business case. *Equality, Diversity, and Inclusion: An International Journal*, 29(5), 413–421.

Bourke, J. and Espedido, A. (2019). Why inclusive leaders are good for organizations, and how to become one. *Harvard Business Review*, 2–5.

Brimhall, K.C. (2019). Inclusion is important... But how do I include? Examining the effects of leader engagement on inclusion, innovation, job satisfaction, and perceived quality of care in a diverse nonprofit healthcare organization. *Nonprofit and Voluntary Sector Quarterly*, 48(4), 716–737.

Chen, C. and Tang, N. (2018). Does perceived inclusion matter in the workplace? *Journal of Managerial Psychology*, 33(1), 43–57.

Colquitt, J.A., Lepine, J.A., Wesson, M.J. (eds) (2017). Teams: Characteristics and diversity. In *Organizational Behavior: Improving Performance and Commitment in the Workplace*. McGraw-Hill, New York.

Du Brin, A.J. (2016). Cultural diversity and cross-cultural organizational behavior. In *Fundamentals of Organizational Behavior*, Du Brin, A.J. (ed.). Academic Media Solutions, Solon.

Farndale, E., Biron, M., Briscoe, D.R., Raghuram, S. (2015). A global perspective on diversity and inclusion in work organizations. *The International Journal of Human Resource Management*, 26(6), 677–687.

Feintzeig, R. (2020). Diversity is a higher priority. Now what? *The Wall Street Journal*, 13.

Ferdman, B.M. and Deane, B. (2014). *Diversity at Work: The Practice of Inclusion*. John Wiley and Sons, New York.

Goodman, N.R. (2013). Taking diversity and inclusion initiatives global. *Industrial and Commercial Training*, 45(3), 180–183.

Gowan, M. and Lepak, D. (2020). *Human Resource Management: Managing Employees for Competitive Advantage*. Chicago Business Press, Saint Charles.

Gulati, R., Mayo, A.J., Nohria, N. (2017). *Management: An Integrated Approach*. Cengage, Boston.

Holger, D. (2019). The business case for more diversity. *The Wall Street Journal*, 11.

Hunt, V., Layton, D., Prince, S. (2014). Why diversity matters. Report, McKinsey and Company, London.

Irvine, A. and Lupart, J. (2008). Into the workforce: Employers' perspectives of inclusion. *Developmental Disabilities Bulletin*, 36, 225–250.

Jones, G.R. and George, J.M. (eds) (2019). *Essentials of Contemporary Management*. McGraw-Hill, New York.

Jordan, T.H. (2011). Moving from diversity to inclusion. *Profiles in Diversity Journal*, 22, 1–3.

Kinicki, A. and Williams, B.K. (2020). *Management*. McGraw-Hill, New York.

Krentz, M., Dean, J., Garcia-Alonso, J., Brooks Taplett, F., Tsusaka, M., Vaughn, E. (2019). *Fixing the Flawed Approach to Diversity*. Boston Consulting Group, New York.

Linares, C.E. (2020). Latinos first generation in the workplace: Perception of diversity and inclusion. *SAM Advanced Management Journal*, 83(4), 54.

Neck, C.P. and Houghton, J.D. (2020). *Organizational Behavior: A Skill-Building Approach*. Sage, London.

Oswick, C. and Noon, M. (2014). Discourses of diversity, equality, and inclusion: Trenchant formulations of transient fashions? *British Journal of Management*, 25, 23–29.

Pasztor, S.K. (2019). Exploring the framing of diversity rhetoric in "Top-rated in Diversity" organizations. *International Journal of Business Communication*, 56(4), 455–475.

Pitman, R. (2019). The power of knowing. *Strategic Finance*, 17–18.

Riccò, R. and Guerci, M. (2014). Diversity challenge: An integrated process to bridge the implementation gap. *Business Horizons*, 57(2), 235–245.

Robbins, S.P. and Judge, T.A. (eds) (2017). *Organizational Behavior*. Pearson, London.

Sabharwal, M. (2014). Is diversity management sufficient? Organizational inclusion to further performance. *Public Personnel Management*, 43(2), 197–217.

Samosh, D. (2020). The benefits of inclusion: Disability and work in the 21st century. *Discussion View Thread – Social Issues in Management*, 1–3.

Sanyal, C., Wilson, D., Sweeney, C., Rachele, J.S., Kaur, S., Yates, C. (2015). Diversity and inclusion depend on effective engagement. *Human Resource Management International Digest*, 23(5), 21–24.

Sardon, M. and Holger, D. (2019). What holds firms back. *The Wall Street Journal*, 14.

Schawbel, D. (2012). How companies can benefit from inclusion. *Entrepreneurs*, 14, 1–4.

Sherbin, L. and Rashid, R. (2017). Diversity doesn't stick without inclusion. *Harvard Business Review*, 1–5.

Shore, L.M., Randel, A.E., Chung, B.G., Dean, M.A., Holcombe Ehrhart, K., Singh, G. (2011). Inclusion and diversity in work groups: A review and model for future research. *Journal of Management*, 37(4), 1262–1289.

Sinha, V. (2019). Diversity need not be a mere buzzword. *Washington Business Journal*, 67.

Steele, R. and Derven, M. (2015). Diversity and inclusion and innovation: A virtuous cycle. *Industrial and Commercial Training*, 47(1), 1–7.

Tang, N., Jiang, Y., Chen, C., Zhou, Z., Chen, C.C., Yu, Z. (2015). Inclusion and inclusion management in the Chinese context: An exploratory study. *The International Journal of Human Resource Management*, 26(6), 856–874.

Thompson, L.L. (ed.) (2008). *Organizational Behavior Today*. Pearson/Prentice Hall, New York.

Weber, L. (2019). Inside Eli Lilly's diversity effort. *The Wall Street Journal*, 8.

Whitelaw, C. (2016). Developing an inclusive perspective for a diverse college: Inclusion = diversity + engagement. *Integral Review*, 12(1), 32–64.

6

A Solidarity Economy Group Implementing Inclusive Recruitment Within a Territory

After several decades of fighting against exclusion and discrimination in employment, France has demonstrated its commitment to inclusion in this field. The concept of inclusion is now widely used in many reference texts on employment policy. "Let's give ourselves the means for inclusion": this is the title of the report submitted on January 16, 2018, by Jean-Marc Borello (president of the SOS group) to Muriel Pénicaud (Minister of Labor), who retained a few recommendations from this report, including the creation of a fund for inclusion in employment (circular of January 31, 2019).

An Inclusion Employment Council (*Conseil de l'inclusion dans l'emploi* (CIE)) was also created in November 2018 (replacing the *Conseil national de l'insertion par l'activité économique* (CNIAE)) and placed under the Minister of Labor to develop proposals on inclusion. The mission that this council has given itself was clarified by Thibaut Guilluy, president of the CIE: "Together, we must enable all persons who encounter particular difficulties to be able to regain their autonomy and dignity through work."

Reading these texts leads us to define inclusion in employment as a process by which actions are undertaken collectively by the actors in a territory in order to co-construct a professional environment accessible to all and to allow any person who is far from a professional activity, because of

---

Chapter written by Rahma CHEKKAR and Renaud CHENON.

their situation or specific problems, to have lasting access to it, regardless of their level of qualification.

The issue of developing territorial inclusion dynamics is openly declared to be a major issue in France. In a circular, the government details "the operational deployment methods for the plan to mobilize 10,000 companies for inclusion in employment and those of the PAQTE (Pact with Neighborhoods for All Businesses)" (circular of February 4, 2019). Initiatives aimed at inclusion in employment were also promoted during the sixth edition of the Day of Territorial Initiatives for Employment (JITE) organized by the Ministry of Labor on June 27, 2019, in Paris and on the occasion of which a new space made its appearance: the "inclusion crossroads". On September 10, 2019, the president of the CIE officially handed over the "Pact of Ambition for Insertion through Economic Activity – Enabling Everyone to Find Their Place" (known as the IAE Pact of Ambition) to Muriel Pénicaud in the presence of the President of the French Republic, Emmanuel Macron. During this official launch, a discussion period called an "inclusion village" highlighted numerous initiatives and projects for employment in the heart of the territories.

The evolution of the institutional framework immediately raises the question of how to implement inclusion in employment at a practical level: how can it be implemented in organizations? How can it be promoted in the territories? The aim of our research is to provide some answers to these questions by looking into the "black box" that is the process of implementing inclusion on a practical level in employment in organizations and in the territories. To shed light on this process, we have chosen to draw inspiration from the responses provided by "organizations that mobilize neglected human resources", which include social and solidarity economy (SSE) structures, but which are nevertheless little highlighted in the previous literature (Davister et al. 2004; Defourny and Nyssens 2011; Gianfaldoni and Morand 2015; Tantely Ranjatoelina and Zaoual 2016).

More specifically, we are interested in one of the answers provided by the national SSE federation known as COORACE (this acronym originally stood for *coordination des associations d'aide aux chômeurs par l'emploi* (Coordination of Associations Helping the Unemployed through Employment")), namely the spin-off and dissemination of an innovative recruitment method called Vita Air. This method was acclaimed at the inclusion village (mentioned above) where it was presented by one of the authors of this chapter, speaking as an ambassador for COORACE and also as the director of one of the few organizations that have already experimented with this method. More specifically, this is the solidarity economy grouping ISA Groupe, which we use to describe and understand the process of implementing the Vita Air method and, more broadly, the inclusion of human resources neglected by SSE actors in its area of intervention.

The research reported in this chapter aims to understand a little-explored phenomenon (Dumez 2013) and is part of an inductive (Thomas 2006) and exploratory (Charreire-Petit and Durieux 2007) approach based on a single case (Dyer and Wilkins 1991), namely that of ISA Groupe. The choice of this case is explained by two main reasons: (1) it is undeniably methodological opportunism insofar as one of the authors is the current director of the group at the heart of our research; and (2) beyond the easy access to data, the case studied constitutes an exemplary case (Yin 2003) of the phenomenon studied: ISA Groupe is a grouping composed of several structures of integration through economic activity (SIAEs) which, by proposing a work situation and socio-professional support to people in difficulty (Gardin et al. 2012), is the bearer of projects for an inclusive society. We rely on primary data from "complete participant observation" (Adler 1987) by one of the authors. The distance of the observer (subject of the phenomenon studied) was ensured by collaboration with a non-observer researcher and by the mobilization of secondary data (speeches, press, reports and other support).

This chapter is organized as follows. Section 6.1 presents the Vita Air methodology. Section 6.2 provides details about ISA Groupe and its commitment to inclusion in employment. Section 6.3 looks at the changes in the way the group operates as a result of the Vita Air implementation. Section 6.4 looks back at the long process of ISA Groupe's implementation of this method.

6.1. Vita Air, a recruitment method for inclusion

The Vita Air method originates from reflection and work initiated by COORACE in the mid-2000s.

6.1.1. *Background to the development of the Vita Air method*

In order to support "the emergence of projects promoting economic development and solidarity in the territories", in 2005, COORACE launched a process called Vita whose objective was to "enhance integration in the territories through cooperation of actors".

In this context, all of COORACE's member organizations (more than 500) were invited to reflect on and propose projects that work towards more inclusive territories in terms of employment. Among all the projects presented in 2006, we were particularly interested in the one proposed by Air (based in Parthenay in the Deux-Sèvres department), which aimed to reexamine the enterprises' recruitment processes in order to encourage exchanges between the SIAEs and the companies in their territory of intervention. Air proposed to develop a structured recruitment method involving the actors in the territorial ecosystem, in particular employing structures. During several working sessions (from 2006 to 2008), the project presented by Air was the subject of collective reflection. The exchanges held during these meetings enabled Air's director to develop his recruitment method project and to experiment with it within his group from 2010. Reflection on dissemination of the method then took over.

6.1.2. *Foundations, principles and diffusion of the Vita Air method*

This method is called Vita Air, a juxtaposition of Vita (from the name of the approach) and Air (from the name of the association that created the method). It originated from the desire to address several issues: the recruitment requirements set by the employing structures are more focused on qualification criteria (diplomas) than on skills criteria; given the sometimes "over-dimensioned" nature of the recruitment criteria, the employing structures encounter recruitment difficulties (even more so in rural areas) due to a lack of candidates with the required qualifications; hence the need to think about solutions to compensate for these shortcomings in the recruitment process. Many jobseekers, enrolled in integration programs, have proven skills but cannot (and/or do not wish to) engage in a process of overqualification.

The Air association's project aimed to encourage employers to reexamine their recruitment processes and to become aware of the added value of recruiting these jobseekers for integration in both their organization and their territory. To this end, Air offers personalized support to employment structures: on the one hand, so that they can adapt workstations to jobseekers registered in an integration process (taking into account their specific problems) who have the required skills, but not necessarily the qualifications mentioned on the job vacancy sheets; on the other hand, so that they can enhance the technical skills of their current employees who do not have the required qualifications, but who have proven skills for the positions being recruited. The aim is to encourage internal recruitment in order to free up positions requiring basic skills that some people have mastered through an insertion process, so that they can be put in a professional situation.

To this end, the Vita Air method includes three phases: a diagnostic phase aimed at assisting the territory's potential employers in identifying their needs (current or future) in terms of jobs and skills; a construction phase for a service offer based on the results of the diagnostic phase in identifying their needs (current or future) in terms of jobs by finely defining these needs in terms of tasks and skills; and a phase of building a service offer based on the results of the said diagnosis and aiming, among other things, to enhance the skills of job seekers in a territorial perspective involving forward-looking management of jobs and skill.

The diagnosis provided for in the Vita Air model can concern one or more workstations. This diagnosis of workstations comprises four phases (Figure 6.1) and is the subject of an agreement signed between the potential employer and the SIAE that proposes to implement the approach within it.

This approach, carried out free of charge in the desired employing structures, also enables the SIAEs to deepen their knowledge of workstations, gain skills, develop their HR expertise and become more professional in this area: they will thus be able to provide HR advice (optimizing performance through the integration of jobseekers) and offer support in employment. Although it was designed and tested by Air Services, this method is intended to be widely disseminated and used by social organizations with inclusive intentions. Therefore, one of COORACE's missions is to encourage implementation of the Vita Air method, in particular by its members.

Study stage	Deployment phase	Results analysis stage	Restitution stage
▶ Interview with the manager with the help of an interview questionnaire to understand how the business operates and to identify recruitment problems. ▶ Interview with the team or workshop manager involved with the positions identified as problematic. ▶ Interview with an employee in each post involved.	▶ Evaluating the business' production line. ▶ Breaking down positions identified as problematic into tasks ▶ Breaking down tasks (even "secondary" ones) into skills, distinguishing specific technical skills and skills that do not require qualifications ▶ Identifying losses in the production chain	▶ Identifying strong points, weak points and areas of development that can be envisaged in the production chain ▶ Highlighting added value where tasks are segmented and providing a rationale for positions requiring qualifications ▶ Evaluating risks	▶ Meeting with the manager to discuss the results of the enquiry, to identify points of agreement and possible points to adjust to write accurate job descriptions ▶ Collegial discussion to define an experimental method of organization and potentially an implementation calendar

Figure 6.1. *Overview of the four phases of workstation diagnosis*

The Vita Air method, protected by a trademark registration (INPI registration 4767531604135), has thus been the subject of a spin-off begun in several COORACE member insertion structures. In order to pursue and accelerate this spin-off, the Vita Air project has been integrated into the social innovation accelerator (SIA) set up and run by the *Agence nouvelle des solidarités actives* (Ansa), whose role is to support and evaluate implementation of the Vita Air method in the spin-off structures.

6.2. ISA Groupe: Its organization and its culture in favor of inclusion

Among the organizations that have experimented with the Vita Air method is ISA Groupe, a solidarity economy group based in Aubigny-sur-Nère in the French department of Cher.

6.2.1. *ISA Groupe's adoption of a transversal functional structure*

The embryonic form of ISA Groupe was an association that was created on October 19, 1987, and began its activity of providing staff on January 1, 1988, under the status of an intermediary association (IA), like many integration structures at that time marked by the arrival of mass unemployment and the Seguin law of July 23, 1987: this law gave a status (that of IAs) to many initiatives that already existed but which were not necessarily structured.

Initially, IAs were not restricted in their activity of making personnel available. Following lobbying, especially by temporary work companies, and the intervention of the legislator, IAs can no longer make personnel available to companies for more than 3 consecutive months. The people in charge of administering the historical IAs, which are now called ISA Services, in 1995 created another association with the business of providing temporary work: this second association is now called ISA Intérim.

Following the law against exclusion of July 29, 1998, which aims to place people in work integration, they must have approval from Pôle Emploi. A third temporary work integration association was then created, which is now called ISA 2i and manages all candidates who have the aforesaid approval (ISA Intérim continues to manage candidates who do not have such approval). Then, in 2002, a work integration site was created. In response to a need in the region, the Sancerre Sologne country union considered creating a structure offering its services to local authorities (particularly in terms of riverbank maintenance, rivers and various green spaces) and suggested to those in charge of administering ISA entities that they carry out this structure, which is now known as ISA Entraide.

Since his arrival in 2002, the group's current director has been in charge of the three integration structures: ISA Services, ISA 2i and ISA Entraide. The association ISA Intérim was, for its part, directed at that time by another person. The cohabitation of two distinct managements (as well as of three distinct presidents at the head of the four associations) was a source of conflict in 2008 resulting from visions and strategic orientations that had diverged over time. It was not until a few years later that it was decided that one and the same person would be in charge of managing all four previously independent structures and that one and the same person would assume the role of president of the four structures.

In 2015, ISA Groupe was created as the parent structure (with a board composed of seven directors), to which all the abovementioned associative entities are attached. The same year, two other entities were created within the group: the ISA GE association, which is the employers' group that provides all the permanent employees made available to the group's other structures according to their needs, and the ISA Mutualisation association, which is in charge of collective purchasing for the group. Finally, in 2018, an integration company, ISA Partenaire, was created to take charge of certain activities that had recently been set up (industrial subcontracting, waterless vehicle washing). Currently, ISA Groupe is composed of seven associative entities with distinct activities.

Since 2015, the group has also expanded its range of services and offers a broader, more diversified and complementary range of services to companies, local authorities and associations in the region (supporting and providing personnel for missions of varying duration, various services and subcontracting), private individuals (personal services) and jobseekers (social and professional support, enhancement and development of their skills through training and work experience). At the same time, the group is organized into nine divisions in which permanent employees work: management division; development division; service offering division; reception division; skills division; social support division; project division; communication division; HR accounting division.

As regards integration activities, the group is financially supported by the Cher departmental council and the DIRECCTE (Cher territorial unit), which both grant it operating subsidies (aid for integration posts). The group also benefits from the support of the Centre-Val de Loire regional council (funding linked to projects that transit via the Sancerre-Sologne country union). Apart from these few subsidies, ISA Groupe has chosen to be independent of public funding: the group is more than 90% self-financing thanks to the development of its activities.

6.2.2. *ISA Groupe's reinforcement of its culture of inclusion*

The group, which is committed to the SSE and more specifically to integrating jobseekers in the Sancerre-Sologne territory, works on a daily basis with a concern for social cohesion and territorial cohesion to match people who are looking for employees for their business with those who are unemployed.

For several years, ISA Groupe has been committed to an approach that promotes inclusion in employment with the added motivation of acting in a regional dynamic. ISA Groupe is in fact a local organization that is part of the dynamics of territorial development and participates actively in the implementation of inclusion public policies. The culture of inclusion within the group is reflected in three fundamental values that have been adopted, internalized and put into practice across all its activities and which ISA Groupe communicates: consideration and respect for the individual – the group strives to take into account the individual in their uniqueness and in their relationships with others, based on the principle that each person is a source of wealth in the making; solidarity – the group aims to support people in building their social and professional partnerships and projects, with a view to enhancing the skills and competencies of each person for the benefit of the region; the development of solidarity territories – the group aspires to create territorial dynamics to encourage social links and economic cooperation to better meet the needs of all for the benefit of all.

This culture has been reinforced by the creation of a slogan that explains the group's inclusive and collective approach as well as its desire to involve all players in creating jobs in the group's territory: "Together, let's create jobs." This slogan is the result of collective work carried out in the presence of administrators, management and employee representatives from 2010 onwards with a view to the restructuring as an associative group. During the working groups, naturally, the words "employment" and "together" were proposed. Questioning emerged about integrating the concept of "territory" in the slogan. The idea of "creating jobs together" (implicitly with the territory's economic actors and jobseekers) triumphed and reflects the group's mission quite well.

ISA Groupe's management also constantly communicates both internally and externally about the inclusive culture as a means of cementing identity:

"Jobseekers, before they have administrative status, are first and foremost a sum of skills" (speech at the inclusion village on September 10, 2019).

6.3. ISA Groupe, from a reactive to a proactive inclusive approach

ISA Groupe officially took hold of the Vita Air method in 2015. In line with the Otop system presented by Urasadettan (2015), the Vita Air method invites SIAEs to abandon the cult of the diploma (Bruna et al. 2017), to which French companies seem to be very attached, to develop a culture of competence and then to propagate this culture in companies in their respective territories. As part of the process of appropriating and implementing this method, the group was consequently led to modify its functioning and change its position.

6.3.1. Support aimed at ensuring candidates are proactive in their approach

The implementation of Vita Air led ISA Groupe to adjust its internal organization: before this method was implemented, the vocational integration counselors (*conseillers en insertion professionnelle* (CIPs)) were each in charge of a portfolio of candidates that they managed from start to finish, in other words, from reception to prospecting. The disadvantage of this system is that the CIPs were sometimes led to neglect certain aspects of the support, to the detriment of jobseekers, if they were overloaded with work in one of their many activities.

Since the implementation of Vita Air, the group has operated differently: candidates continue to benefit from individual support, but are first welcomed by the "skills development center" (*pôle déclinaison des compétences* (PDC)), whether or not they have Pôle Emploi approval. During an initial interview, the objective is to collect all the classic elements needed to validate their registration and then to make an initial assessment of their personal situation: in particular, this involves highlighting all the skills they have acquired in the course of their life at the time of their registration. Even if the majority of jobseekers come to ISA Groupe because it is fairly well identified in its territory as a player in the employment market and as being potentially able to find them a job, the approach adopted by ISA Groupe also consists of making candidates aware that they have many skills that are valuable and may be valued by companies independently of their situation and their specific, often complex, problems.

At this stage of the support process, the PDC professionals have a vision of the candidate's situation at a given moment. They then discuss with professionals from the Social Support Unit (*pôle accompagnement social* (PAS)) to determine whether the candidate needs to be monitored by their unit. If so, the candidate is supported by the PAS in order to work on the employment obstacles identified. Once these obstacles have been removed, the candidate is welcomed back by the SDC, which approaches the Service Offer Center (*pôle offre de services* (POS)) to consider putting the candidate in a work situation. At the end of this work placement, the client company issues a "certificate of competence" to the employee made available by ISA Groupe.

In addition, each interview with the PDC or PAS gives rise to a "reciprocal commitment", which consists of defining with the candidate what both parties must do until the next meeting: something must happen between two interviews on the part of both the ISA Groupe and the person in integration. For example, if a barrier related to mobility is identified, both parties agree on the actions to be taken to try to overcome this difficulty: the CIPs may, for example, suggest contacting a partner who can make cars available, or offer the candidate four hours of work per week, as this is the minimum working time that allows the financing of the driving license. However, the final decision is up to the candidate. The idea is to make the candidate a player in their professional integration and to make them part of a proactive rather than reactive approach.

Although the introduction of a proactive dynamic into the support provided by ISA Groupe is a fundamental change in position in the implementation of the Vita Air approach, it is not easy to put in place for two reasons: on the one hand, it is not easy to find the candidates actors; on the other hand, the role of the CIP, which is sometimes seen as a "savior" (by the candidates, as well as by the few CIPs suffering from "savior syndrome"). In the paradigm advocated by the Vita Air approach, each proposal from the CIP must be linked to validation by the candidates in the context of a proactive exchange. The role of the CIP is not to make the decision for them, but to help them build a pathway to employment. In any case, this is how the ISA Groupe's management wishes to develop the CIP profession.

When candidates go through the PDC, their skills are assessed and a career path is defined, particularly in terms of the targeted jobs. The skills acquired by the candidates are then compared with the skills required in the targeted job descriptions (and, if applicable, developed as part of the workstation diagnostics). If there is a significant gap between the skills required by the targeted workstations and the verified skills of a candidate, the logical next step in the Vita Air approach is to propose to fill this gap through training. ISA Groupe has not yet set up its own training center (as is the case in other integration structures) and calls upon local training organizations (AFPA, AFPI, etc.) when necessary. In the long term and ideally, ISA Groupe aims to set up ad hoc training courses if no organization in the territory can meet the training needs identified by the PDC. Moreover, the group was designed to be able to add new activities if the opportunity arises and could consider creating "ISA Training", especially since this could create direct jobs if some of the registered candidates have the skills to provide training.

6.3.2. Adopting a proactive approach to developing its activities

Since the implementation of Vita Air, ISA Groupe has allowed itself to think about activities (outside of its historical role as an intermediary) that create direct employment. For a long time, ISA Groupe engaged in traditional business development aimed at creating indirect employment (the group had no control over the jobs created, acting only as a facilitator between supply and demand) by trying to match the needs expressed by people seeking employment, most of whom lived in its area of intervention, with the needs expressed by companies in the same territory. When ISA Groupe was unable to find a candidate who met a job description, it advertised jobs "crossing its fingers" that candidates would take up positions.

With Vita Air, ISA Groupe has completely changed its approach to territorial development. As regards the provision of services, the main change lies in the creation of job diagnostics, which have led the group to meet more with companies in order to better respond to their recruitment needs. As for supply, ISA Groupe has also started to meet more with players in the local ecosystem (by increasing the number of direct meetings, joining networks, taking part in local discussion forums and trying to understand what could be done to help them deal with their day-to-day difficulties). Thus, using a proactive approach, in addition to reexamining companies' recruitment processes, ISA Groupe is interested in the way they operate to improve their daily lives: the need may be expressed by the companies themselves or may emanate from an ISA Groupe employee (e.g. creation of service offers dedicated to managing farewell parties, providing bicycles, manufacturing pallet furniture).

6.3.3. *Adopting an approach that leads actors to give meaning to their interaction*

Implementing the Vita Air model in a territory also means developing actors' capacity to give meaning to their interaction. In addition to developing activities to maintain a comfortable level of self-financing, ISA Groupe aims to develop territorial synergy. Since the creation of Vita Air, ISA Groupe has been trying to develop the capacity of its territory (which has the particularity of being a rural territory) to be self-managing in terms of employment by restricting the development of its activities to a local perimeter and by giving priority to the employment of local people. The idea is to take advantage of the wealth created by one of the actors in the territory to put other actors in the territory in work.

In addition, by helping to increase these people's skills, ISA Groupe is able to put them more easily in professional situations and thus theoretically contribute to increasing their purchasing power and their level of consumption (perhaps even in part in the territory), making it possible to decrease their dependence on social benefits and ultimately reduce the cost to the community.

Participation in discussions on inclusion in employment (within COORACE in particular) and implementation of the Vita Air method have led ISA Groupe to become part of real territorial strategies: while providing services to a number of local stakeholders (support and response to companies' needs; support and development of previously neglected human resources), ISA Groupe is contributing to the development of inclusive local dynamics by using economic levers (creation of economic momentum by involving local economic stakeholders) and by integrating a social dimension (development of solidarity and social links).

For example, behind the pallet furniture manufacturing business, there is a whole circular economy logic: pallets, which are waste products that companies do not know what to do with, become a resource for creating jobs in the territory, enhancing the value of people who are excluded through the know-how that they express by participating in lamp manufacture. Behind the organic market gardening activity, the ISA Groupe's strategy is different and consists of developing more and more cooperation with local actors in order to increase this activity and thus create direct employment. The strategy goes far beyond this, because if ISA Groupe no longer has enough land to satisfy all its new customers, it will have no choice but to rely on the network of local farmers, who will potentially be asked to recruit human resources. In this way, ISA Groupe will create indirect jobs.

ISA Groupe works with many companies. When a client deals with ISA Groupe, it does so because it is in line with its values, has integrated its inclusive intention and is ready to put neglected human resources in a professional situation. Currently, ISA Groupe has over 200 different clients. While a certain number of them are only clients, ISA Groupe has a real appetite to lead its clients to become partners, in other words, actors in this inclusive territorial dynamic. For example, Wilo-Intec, a privileged partner for more than 15 years, has fully embraced the posture underlying the Vita Air approach. Wilo-Intec frequently communicates about its commitment to inclusion in employment and its partnership with ISA Groupe and thus acts as a communication vector on the added value of the Vita Air approach to its network.

6.4. The process by which ISA Groupe implemented the Vita Air method: A long, gradual and consensual process

Although the Vita Air method is now beginning to bear fruit at ISA Groupe and in its territory, it is at the cost of a lengthy process. The case of ISA Groupe suggests that implementation of an innovative recruitment method to promote inclusion in employment – in relation to the SIAEs (and the economic actors in their territory) – is part of a long and progressive process insofar as it imposes profound changes in terms of organizational practices and attitudes. From the perspective of conflict resolution and the fight against the "resistance to change" put forward by Lewin (1946), this process is intended to be consensual (and therefore slow) and, in other words, non-coercive, and it is therefore part of a "group dynamic".

ISA Groupe thus sees the implementation of inclusion in employment as a collective process that implies a collaborative effort in which everyone (employees on integration programs, permanent employees, members of the board of directors; managers, employees and members of the HR department of the employing organizations; funders participating in the discussion as part of management dialogues; training organizations; etc.) is invited to be actors in this change. The process of change implemented by ISA Groupe's management thus follows the path suggested by Lewin (1946) in his planned approach to change (unfreeze, change, refreeze).

6.4.1. *Preparing the ground to implement the model (2006–2012)*

ISA Groupe has always been a member (even in its embryonic form) of COORACE. ISA Groupe's current director therefore had the opportunity to take part in all the collective reflection led by this federation on the Vita Air project. Seduced by the Vita Air approach, a method which had the merit of formalizing practices and which was, moreover, totally in line with his way of thinking, the current director of the group then tried to transfer the model to the ISA entities. He drew on exchanges held during working groups led by COORACE (between 2006 and 2009) and during a visit to Air Services to think about implementing the method within the ISA entities (as a reminder, the group had not yet been created) and started from the idea that it should be easier to raise awareness among administrators, employees and then the players in the territorial ecosystem regarding the interest of setting up inclusive territorial dynamics with a certified method that had already proved its worth at Air Services.

He then prepared the ground by making his employees aware of the philosophy of the Vita Air model – but implicitly, in other words, without referring to the method developed by Air Services – and his desire to transfer this model to the ISA entities. He was thus beginning to integrate the Vita Air philosophy into the development strategies of the entities he managed (in the definition of business plans) to reexamine the operating processes (reception, support of candidates) with his colleagues and to set up reflection, which was necessarily collective, on the evolution of these processes. Without introducing the idea of a preliminary diagnosis of the workstations, the position of the IPC was reexamined during exchanges with its collaborators by raising the following questions in particular: how can employees be valued? How can we enter into a process of permanent valorization? How can ISA entities in the territory move beyond their role as intermediaries and allow themselves to become actors in the territory and thus to be a force for proposals?

Convinced by the added value that implementing the Vita Air method could bring, as it reinforced the certainties that he had already begun to put in place, the ISA Groupe director now had to convince the members of the ISA entities' boards of directors of the interest of integrating the Vita Air logic. Between 2009 and 2012, alone against all, he had to fight his way to get the directors, who did not believe in it at all at the beginning, to understand and integrate the interest that this approach could have for the development of both the group and the territory. While the administrators were quick to measure the added value that the method could bring to the operational part (diagnosis), it was more complicated to get them to assess the added value that the method could bring in terms of territorial strategies and cooperation and mobilization of the territory's actors to work together.

At that time, marked by a drop in business and internal tensions, it was also complicated to make the administrators understand why the director of several ISA entities spent time reflecting, within working groups, on a solution coming from the outside. This was all the more the case as this same director was beginning, in that same period, to infiltrate numerous networks and spaces for reflection: the development council which the Sancerre-Sologne country had set up (he had also been its president since 2008), the CPME du Cher (confederation of small and medium-sized enterprises), the CRESS Centre-Val de Loire and a whole host of organizations in which the group was not necessarily expected, but where it wished to be present to understand how actors in the territorial ecosystem operated.

This external commitment can also play a decisive role in reaffirming partnerships and giving the process credibility. Thus, during this first (unfreeze) phase, the director of the ISA Groupe tried to create motivation for change among the administrators and permanent employees to get them to question their perceptions and habits and reexamine their professional postures and practices. During this phase, there was notable resistance to change, linked in particular to "group norms" (administrators with a traditional vision of a director who must be present to develop the group; some of the CIPs with a traditional vision of their profession).

6.4.2. The time taken to integrate the model (2013–2014)

Between 2013 and 2014, the ISA bodies were committed to the CEDRE quality approach (now called CEDRE ISO) initially developed by COORACE for its members. On this occasion, the bodies' procedures were reviewed, particularly in terms of recruitment. During this work, the dynamics instilled by the Vita Air approach stood out, even though the CEDRE quality approach was initially focused only on reception and support.

The advantage of integrating the Vita Air model is that it adds a whole logic of proactive business relationships to reception and support. At that time, the directors were increasingly convinced that there was added value in implementing the Vita Air approach and so the decision was made to enter this process. At the end of 2014, ISA Group benefited from training (known as "action training") led by the founder of Air Services and the Vita Air method. This training took place in Aubigny-sur-Nère over 3 days. Only the members of the management team, the development team and the skills development team attended the entire training and were therefore really aware of the Vita Air method at the time.

The main difficulty in implementing Vita Air (this is still true today) lies in the need for the people involved in the process (administrators, permanent employees) to be convinced of its added value and to converge in the same direction. The approach was rather well received by the members of the development division (in addition to providing them with a structured and therefore very reassuring operational methodology, it allowed them to move away from a permanent commercial approach to a different approach to development where the relationship with clients and/or partners made sense).

The position of the CIPs was less consensual: some managed to project themselves and quickly perceived the impact that implementation of the method could have on their daily life; others, on the contrary, did not manage, or did not wish, to project themselves by reassuring themselves about the organization they had mastered for years (aware, however, that the implementation of Vita Air would mean re-examining the group's position in the territory and would have an impact on the internal organization). Two profiles emerged of how people reacted and this opposition in approaches is still apparent today. On the one hand, people seduced and convinced of the added value that the approach could bring to the territory appropriated the change in position/approach and integrated into a proactive approach by constantly trying to transform constraints into opportunities. On the other hand, reluctant people expressed the fear of losing the achievements of the current operating mode and the fear of being overworked. They could have also anticipated a possible crisis of professional identity or even have had a top-down conception of management.

As a follow-up to the training that took place at the end of 2014, collective meetings involving all permanent employees, regardless of their division, were organized from 2015 onwards so that they could become immersed in and involved in the Vita Air method. These meetings also aimed to re-think the internal organization and define the organization to be put in place in a collegial manner in order to enter into the logic underlying the Vita Air approach. As an example, during a working group held on April 16, 2015 (which followed other meetings during which an internal organization by activity had been decided upon), it was possible to think about the audiences for which each activity should specialize. More specifically, ISA Groupe works with three audiences: principals (those who place orders for labor or services); candidates (those who come to register but who have not yet been placed in a professional situation); and employees (those who are already registered and have already been placed in a professional situation). One of the outcomes of the working group was the agreement that the development unit would focus solely on the principals and would not have to be in contact with the candidates and employees. Numerous meetings then followed to refine the proposed organization.

Some actors in the territorial ecosystem were informed from the beginning of the approach undertaken during management dialogues: more precisely, the Pôle Emploi employment center and the funders, which were the departmental council of Cher and DIRECCTE (the Cher territorial unit). In general, DIRECCTE was involved whenever ISA Groupe planned to change its internal organization. During these management dialogues, a rather positive action from the funders was noted, in particular from the time Vita Air was implemented.

The director of the ISA Groupe suggested two possible explanations: (1) these actors were particularly keen on thinking about the territory's development and on questioning the recruitment procedures implemented by companies; (2) the change in territorial strategy adopted by ISA Groupe has been concomitant with a very strong increase in activity. Even if no study to date shows that this growth is attributable to the implementation of Vita Air, these actors certainly made the parallel and considered that Vita Air was an extremely interesting device to ensure the increase in activity. Thus, in this phase (change), the minds of the various people involved in the Vita Air implementation process seemed ready for change. New practices were defined, starting with implementation of the CEDRE quality approach. The internal actors involved were associated with the change during training sessions, work groups, collective meetings, etc., and even participated in reflection on and implementation of the inevitable change in the group's internal organization.

6.4.3. *The time of dissemination and legitimization (since 2015)*

To inform the other players in the local ecosystem, in particular the companies, ISA Groupe scheduled information meetings with them, but the companies were unable to find the time to be informed about a subject that may not have seemed important to them. ISA Groupe's development division then contacted and arranged individual meetings with companies, starting with those that were already clients and which ISA Groupe knew to be experiencing recruitment difficulties for certain positions. The work of carrying out the diagnostics provided for in the Vita Air approach thus began in 2015. Feedback from the companies was quite positive because it was an innovative approach in their eyes: the majority of the companies contacted had never been approached from this perspective, i.e. having someone come to meet them only to understand the functioning of the company and to offer to participate free of charge in solving recruitment issues.

In 2017, the group entered a phase of legitimizing and transmitting the Vita Air approach in the local, regional and national scene. In 2017, ISA Groupe applied for a corporate trophy with the aim of legitimizing the approach implemented in companies' eyes because one of the main difficulties encountered by ISA Groupe was its associative status: because of this status, some of the approaches taken by the group were not perceived as credible in the corporate world. Therefore, obtaining a corporate trophy gave ISA Groupe more credibility. ISA Groupe won the second edition of this trophy in the "Stronger Together" category. This recognition was highlighted by COORACE on its website (www.coorace.org): "Congratulations to ISA Groupe, which won the 2nd edition of the 'Creators of the Future' trophies […] in the 'Stronger Together' category! A great award for Vita Air […]."

In 2018, ISA Groupe was a candidate for and winner of a regional SSE award given as part of the SSE month by the CRESS Centre-Val de Loire. This trophy was a way for ISA Groupe to share its experience within the regional SSE network. On the occasion of this recognition, one of the members of this network, in view of the application file presented by ISA Groupe, suggested that ISA Groupe also apply for the SSE initiative prize awarded by Crédit Coopératif. Following its application, ISA Groupe was awarded this prize at the regional level.

Although the group communicated a lot when it won these trophies and prizes, it still communicates about these recognitions through a banner inserted in the signatures of the electronic messages sent by all the employees of the group. It is also worth noting the external professional commitment of the director of ISA Groupe. From his point of view, it is extremely interesting to work on the development of ISA Groupe at the local level and then to go up to the regional and national level in order to communicate about the approach that ISA Groupe has implemented in its territory of intervention and to compare it with what is implemented in other territories. The objective is actually threefold: to promote the position and policy of ISA Groupe; to bring more to other territories; and to enrich the group by learning from other territories' practices. With this triple objective in mind, since 2018, the director of ISA Groupe has taken on the (interim) role of Vita Air ambassador on behalf of COORACE. As such, his role is to promote and communicate the Vita Air approach, to meet organizations that are members of COORACE and to explain to them what the added value of the Vita Air approach can be in their organization and their day-to-day operation, and to represent COORACE in external events related to employment or recruitment for which the Vita Air method may be of interest (working group led by DIRECCTE, territorial unit of Indre; village of inclusion held on September 10, 2019; etc.). As part of the spin-off launched by COORACE and ANSA, the director of ISA Groupe was also asked to train several SIAEs in Vita Air.

Thus, at this stage (refreeze), the new organization implemented and the new working methods developed in line with the Vita Air approach have been adopted by each and every individual (though not necessarily accepted by everyone). To stabilize and consolidate this organization and to prevent old routines from resurfacing, the internal actors have become immersed in the process quickly: contact with the companies involved themselves, systematic mention of the Vita Air approach during meetings, internal and external communication on the implementation of the approach.

6.5. Conclusion

The ISA Groupe case study suggests that, for SIAEs to implement inclusion in employment, there needs to be adoption of a real inclusive culture (or even a profound cultural transformation) accompanied by profound transformations in terms of governance, organization, functioning, practices and posture. The study of this case seems to confirm the main role of leadership in the diffusion of such a culture (Pettigrew 1987). The practical implementation of inclusion in employment by ISA Groupe seems to be based on its leadership's capacity to align and commit all the people involved in its administration (administrators) and in its operation (permanent employees) to the proactive approach to supporting and developing the territory, an approach that underlies the inclusive culture and implementation of Vita Air. In the words of Tantely Ranjatoelina and Zaoual (2016), the implementation of inclusion in employment relies on a "progressively constructed capacity for orchestration".

While our study makes it possible to describe and better understand the process for implementing the Vita Air method, it is complicated to measure its real contribution to the change of approach adopted by certain actors in the territory who work regularly (and increasingly) with ISA Groupe. ISA Groupe seems, for example, to have stimulated a change of behavior in the HR practices of the company Wilo-Intec, but this change of behavior could be attributed to the evolution of the institutional framework in terms of employment in France, as well as to the fact that this company is immersed in an inclusive logic by its membership in a group (Wilo) that is a signatory of the manifesto of the most inclusive companies investing in France.

The ISA Groupe case study, however, seems to suggest that the practical implementation of inclusion in employment by SIAEs, and more broadly by inclusive social organizations, is facilitated by a combination of six factors: (1) governance, financial autonomy and an organization that allows them to seize development opportunities with responsiveness; (2) external commitment and involvement of the leader in the territorial ecosystem; (3) the establishment of a group dynamic throughout the process of implementing the method for inclusion in employment; (4) a permanent concern for consolidating a strong inclusive culture internally and externally; (5) a team specifically dedicated to the development and permanent updating of the portfolio of inclusive activities with the aim of territorial synergy; (6) a team specifically dedicated to the personalized social support of jobseekers and another to their professional support, with particular attention paid to training and skills development.

Inclusive social organizations such as ISA Groupe are trying to contribute to the construction of an inclusive society and to changing the perception of companies with regard to resources that have long been understood as negative (Weppe et al. 2013; Da Fonseca and Bonneveux 2018). ISA Groupe thus invites the managers and members of the HR departments of the companies in its territory to reexamine their recruitment procedures.

6.6. References

Adler, P. (1987). *Membership Roles in Field Research*. Sage, London.

Bruna, M., Montargot, N., Peretti, J. (2017). Point de vue. Les nouveaux chantiers du management de la diversité : quelques pistes de réflexion et de recherche. *Gestion 2000*, 34(5), 433–462.

Charreire-Petit, S. and Durieux, F. (2007). Explorer et tester : les deux voies de la recherche. In *Méthodes de recherche en management*, Thietart, R.A. (ed.). Dunod, Paris.

Da Fonseca, M. and Bonneveux, E. (2018). Responsabilité sociétale de l'entreprise : une étude de la nature et de la valeur perçues des ressources mobilisées dans trois entreprises du secteur de l'imprimerie. *Revue interdisciplinaire management, homme et entreprise*, 32, 45–70.

Davister, C., Defourny, J., Olivier, G. (2004). Les entreprises sociales d'insertion dans l'Union européenne : un aperçu général. *Revue internationale de l'économie sociale*, 293, 24–50.

Defourny, J. and Nyssens, M. (2011). Approches européennes et américaines de l'entreprise sociale : une perspective comparative. *Revue internationale de l'économie sociale*, 319, 18–35.

Dumez, H. (2013). *Méthodologie de la recherche qualitative. Les 10 questions clés de la démarche compréhensive*. Vuibert, Paris.

Dyer, W.G. and Wilkins, A.L. (1991). Better stories, not better constructs, to generate better theory: A rejoinder to Eisenhardt. *Academy of Management Review*, 16(3), 613–619.

Gardin, L., Laville, J.L., Nyssens, M. (eds) (2012). *Entreprise sociale et insertion*. Desclée de Brouwer, Paris.

Gianfaldoni, P. and Morand, P.H. (2015). Incentives, procurement and regulation of work integration social enterprises in France: Old ideas for new firms? *Annals of Public and Cooperative Economics*, 86(2), 199–219.

Lewin, K. (1946). Action research and minority problems. In *Resolving Social Conflict*, Lewin, G.W. (ed.). Harper and Row, London.

Pettigrew, A. (1987). Context and action in the transformation of the firm. *Journal of Management Studies*, 24(6), 649–667.

Tantely Ranjatoelina, J. and Zaoual, A.R. (2016). Inclure des ressources délaissées. *Revue française de gestion*, 25(5), 121–138.

Thomas, D.R. (2006). A general inductive approach for analyzing qualitative evaluation data. *American Journal of Evaluation*, 27(2), 237–246.

Urasadettan, J. (2015). La diffusion de la logique compétence au sein des structures d'insertion : une analyse en termes d'étendue du découplage, le cas de la constitution d'une gestion territorialisée de l'emploi. *La revue des sciences de gestion*, 275–276.

Weppe, X., Warnier, V., Lecocq, X. (2013). Ressources stratégiques, ressources ordinaires et ressources négatives : pour une reconnaissance de l'ensemble du spectre des ressources. *Revue française de gestion*, 234, 43–63.

Yin, R.K. (2003). *Case Study Research: Design and Methods*. Sage, Thousand Oaks.

7

The Role of Social Economy Entrepreneurs in Governing Inclusive Social Innovation Ecosystems: The Cause of Mobility for Vulnerable People in Lorraine

Since the beginning of the millennium, because of the weaknesses and limits of policies that only promote innovation from the perspective of economic development, territories have been emphasizing social innovation as responses to needs expressed by particular social groups that are not met, or even recognized, by markets and public institutions (Moulaert 2009; Richez-Battesti et al. 2012). In particular, they aim to promote the inclusion of people or social groups who are marginalized because, for example, of their age, disability, origins or resources. This is what the region in the east of France is doing, for example, in formulating its economic strategy by supporting volunteering, associative activities and social entrepreneurs.

The reasons for this emphasis are multiple. First of all, territories wish to pursue sustainable development objectives in all their dimensions, whether economic, environmental or social (Djellal and Gallouj 2009). Second, the needs taken into account by social innovation emerge from locally rooted and interacting actors. Indeed, this type of innovation frequently results from intentional, bottom-up processes (Celle 2019).

Chapter written by Paul MULLER, Bérangère SZOSTAK and Delphine WANNENMACHER.

Finally, social innovation promotes the development of new capacities in territories (Moulaert and Sekia 2003; Swyngedouw 2005). In particular, these are those aimed at promoting and developing more inclusive territories, i.e. built not only to meet the needs expressed by specific social groups but also co-constructed with them (Klein et al. 2019).

In addition, public policies emphasize the importance of entrepreneurial activities, understood as interactions between economic agents in a particular socio-cultural context (Zahra and Nambisan 2012; Nambisan and Baron 2013). They are likely to contribute to territorial development, as they promote resource and knowledge flows (Surie 2017; Muller et al. 2020) through the creation of socio-economic networks (Dedehayir et al. 2018). Moreover, entrepreneurs are seen as sources of creativity and innovation. To this end, we adopt a processual approach to entrepreneurship (Gartner 1985).

Taking into account the territorial and entrepreneurial dimensions in the development processes of social innovations motivates adoption of the conceptual framework of the creative territory (Cohendet et al. 2010; Capdevila et al. 2017). The latter emphasizes the existence of three economic strata: the upperground, the underground and the middleground. Businesses are considered to play a key role when it comes to recombining and valorizing original ideas coming from specific communities in the upperground; these ideas sometimes come from isolated and discrete individuals from the underground whose needs may not be covered by market mechanisms and public actors. This theoretical framework seems to us to be particularly well suited to analyzing the production of social innovations by highlighting interactions between the different stakeholders: entrepreneurs, beneficiaries and other actors, whether they are individuals (volunteers, activists, etc.) or organizations, public or private.

Nevertheless, the literature on entrepreneurship mainly deals with innovation and economic value creation problems. The social dimension of innovations, which is the subject of this chapter, is little discussed, which makes it difficult to understand the extent to which business can promote social innovations aimed at the inclusion of vulnerable people. The main objective of this contribution is therefore to understand how entrepreneurial activities allow the social dimension to be included in the development of innovations in the territory. This leads us to question the role of entrepreneurs in the social innovation process. This goes beyond the entrepreneur's role as a creative actor (Kirzner 2009). In particular, we will study their role in governance (Moulaert and Sekia 2003). To this end, we return to social innovation, and then describe the contribution of the creative territory framework for understanding its creation process and specify the role of middleground activities within it. Our questions lead us to explore an entrepreneurial project on the mobility of vulnerable people in Lorraine, which is a region in the east of France. This analysis leads us to think about governance through intermediation, to which businesses contribute.

7.1. Conceptual framework

In this section, we present a review of the literature on the production of social innovations, social innovation within creative territories and the role of entrepreneurs in the production of social innovation.

7.1.1. *The production of social innovations*

According to several authors (Moulaert 2009; Richez-Battesti and Vallade 2009; Lethielleux and Paturel 2017), social innovation responds to an unmet or poorly met social need in a specific space. It occupies a space left vacant by markets and by state institutions and brings into interaction partners who have not had any social connection, or only little, until then. This requires new modes of organization, both institutional and social. From this perspective, social changes can occur, resulting in economic, technological and ecological impacts, depending on the nature of the need to be met, on the actors involved and the space concerned.

This research illustrates what Lethielleux and Paturel (2017) formalize in their analysis (Figure 7.1). The emergence of the idea of the solidarity garage stemmed from identifying a significant problem related to the mobility of vulnerable people. Its development required trial and error, adjustments made in cooperation with the beneficiaries of the service in order to best meet need. Finally, the innovation was appropriated by the stakeholders: vulnerable people, clients and partners, including the traditional garage.

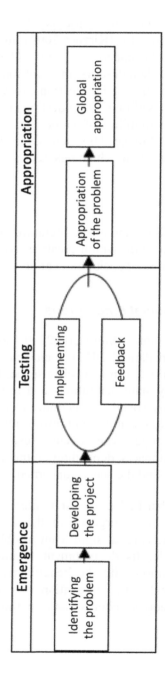

Figure 7.1. *Development of social innovation according to Lethielleux and Paturel (2017, p.10)*

This leads us to examine three major characteristics of social innovation (Muller 2021).

First, its objective is above all to improve the living conditions of the social groups involved by providing solutions adapted to their needs and problems and thus to fully include them in their living space. This implies that it cannot be based solely on an isolated product or service but on a global solution, which may involve a set of adapted products and/or services.

Second, as the main purpose of social innovations is not economic, "traditional" economic actors (public and for-profit structures) are not necessarily able to respond satisfactorily to the need expressed, either because there are no sufficiently profitable perspectives or because the nature of the need is such that it is impossible to propose an appropriate response. This does not mean, however, that public or for-profit structures are totally absent from the process of developing social innovations. They can support them, for example, through subsidies or sponsorship (sponsorship of skills, provision of personnel, etc.). Moreover, in a context of dwindling public funding, organizations developing social innovations may be encouraged to engage in commercial activities to sell goods and services (Le Velly 2008).

Third, social innovations are, by their very nature, the result of collective processes requiring the collaboration of the public concerned, which has the advantage of including them in the process formalized by Lethielleux and Paturel (2017). In addition, it often leads to a questioning of the socio-economic rules, and even of the dominant collective mental models in the environments concerned. The question that arises is how to develop social innovations that promote the inclusion of vulnerable people. As social innovation is embedded in a socio-economic context, our response consists, first of all, in better understanding the environment in which it develops, an environment that we understand through the prism of the creative territory.

7.1.2. Social innovation within creative territories

In order to better understand the development of social innovation for the inclusion of vulnerable people, we consider the territory in which it develops, a territory that can be understood with the creative territory model. Inspired by the work of Florida (Stolarick and Florida 2006), this model distinguishes between the contributions of different economic levels to creative activities and processes: the uppergound, the middleground and the underground (Cohendet et al. 2010; Capdevila et al. 2017).

The upperground concerns all public and private actors considered to be institutional (Simon 2009). This is the primary level for the economic valorization of innovations, in the market sense of the term. It can also be the institutionalization of a social innovation taken over by the State or the market. Here, we find traditional institutions (governments, communities, training and research organizations, etc.), as well as commercial businesses, whether for-profit or not.

Conversely, the underground is made up of individuals who may be amateur artists, activists, volunteers and, more broadly, people who are forces of proposal (Fisher and Amabile 2011). They contribute to the creative bubbling that gives rise to new ideas, especially in the subject at hand, namely ideas for meeting needs, which may or not be met by the market and public institutions. This level is characterized by creative activities that take place outside of any formal organization linked to a market or institutional activity or even "in garages". The activities carried out in the underground are marked by a strong militant dimension while benefiting from a greater latitude for experimentation. Some actors even defend utopias or new visions of society, with, for example, more freedom, equality and fraternity. The activities that are carried out there emphasize discovery and exploration, which leads to a regular search for new solutions to a problem, as well as to experimentation with these solutions and risk-taking (March 1991). The counterpart of the creative autonomy of individuals in the underground lies in their difficulty valorizing their ideas economically through market and organizational mechanisms.

The middleground is positioned between the upperground and the underground. It selects and aggregates certain creative ideas coming from the underground, ideas that are considered useful, in our case, at the social level. The objective is to translate these ideas from the underground into businesses for economic valorization within the upperground (Sarazin et al. 2017). The middleground is characterized, like the upperground, by the collective dimension of the activities carried out there (Mehouachi et al. 2017) within communities, associations, clubs, etc. The diffusion of creative ideas occurs through interactions between economic agents in the context of entrepreneurial activities (Muller et al. 2020). Such activities develop within places and spaces that form platforms that are respectively physical (artists' houses, fablabs, neighborhood houses) and cognitive (very small businesses, especially with associative status). There are also one-off events (neighborhood or village festivals, local competitions) and projects (renewal of city policy neighborhoods, etc.) (Grandadam et al. 2013; Dechamp and Szostak 2016). The question that then arises is: in what way do entrepreneurial activities participate in the development of social innovations in the framework of analysis by creative territories?

7.1.3. *The role of entrepreneurs in producing social innovation*

For the purposes of this chapter, we have adopted a processual approach to entrepreneurship (Gartner 1988; Lamine et al. 2015). Entrepreneurship is considered as a dynamic, emergent phenomenon. It pits the entrepreneur(s) (individual or collective) against their environment, consisting of the institutional and socio-economic framework of their business, as well as the various stakeholders involved (clients and beneficiaries, suppliers, interest groups, competitors, etc.). The analysis focuses on entrepreneurial activities and how they organize the succession of different stages in the business process over time (Langley et al. 2013).

The processual approach seems to us to be particularly appropriate for understanding the role of the entrepreneur insofar as the latter is conceived as a driver of creativity. The entrepreneur is seen as the bearer of not only economic but also social dynamism at the level of structures (Hjorth et al. 2018), sectors of activity and territories (Dutraive et al. 2018). Indeed, the process approach goes beyond the more classical understanding of entrepreneurship, which focuses essentially on the economic and market dimension (Swedberg 2006). Moreover, it introduces the idea that the entrepreneur is not only subject to their environment but also participates in changing it (Sarasvathy et al. 2008). The processual approach emphasizes entrepreneurs' ability to transgress the limits imposed by the existing institutional framework (Hjorth 2017), particularly through the formulation of radically new ideas through novel recombinations of available resources (Héraud and Muller 2017).

Nevertheless, although the entrepreneur has long been identified as being at the origin of innovations, we defend the idea that they can also be a central element of the governance of the collective processes by which innovations are produced. Indeed, the entrepreneur manages to reconcile the top-down (Saebi et al. 2019) and bottom-up (Gupta et al. 2003) logics usually associated with their production in the literature. To this end, they participate in a mechanism that we describe as governance through intermediation, i.e. by playing the role of intermediaries between the different levels (under-, middle- and upperground), as well as between different categories of actors (beneficiaries, activists, private structures, whether part of the social economy or not, and public structures). Howells's approach (2006, p. 720) is generally accepted in the literature. Intermediation refers to "an organization acting as an agent or broker in any aspect of the innovation process between two or more parties". In the case of social innovation production, we consider that the intermediation role of entrepreneurial activities consists of activating different middleground mechanisms (places, spaces, events, projects), which may be an exploitation of the contingencies that entrepreneurs face, as well as of the resources at their disposal.

If we relate this to the different logics by which social innovations are produced, we consider that they may emanate from the upperground or from the underground. According to a first logic, qualified as top-down, the organizations of the upperground, whether they are for-profit or not, play a role in initiating social innovations according to a particular perspective. These innovations are responses to identified opportunities linked to social problems (housing, financial insecurity, etc.). The advantage of the top-down logic is that social innovations benefit from a capacity for large-scale diffusion within socio-economic systems due to their embedding in existing socio-economic systems (Tracey and Stott 2017). However, their social impact may be limited by the expectations of their funders, whose objectives and rationales may be in tension with those of the beneficiaries (Eynaud and Mourey 2015; Raedersdorf 2018). Another limitation lies in the possible distancing between the spaces in which social innovation is designed and the real needs of the populations concerned. In other words, there is a great risk that the social value of the innovation is created for the beneficiaries, rather than with them (Saebi et al. 2019). This is also likely to limit their inclusiveness, as the adequacy of solutions to the real problems faced by the people involved is not guaranteed.

A second logic, described as bottom-up, emanates from the underground. In this context, social innovations emanate from populations or entrepreneurs directly confronted with the existence of social needs that need to be addressed. They aim to find local solutions to local problems and needs. They therefore involve the development and implementation of small-scale experiments (Seyfang and Smith 2007). As close as possible to the target populations, this approach favors the co-construction of innovations with them (Younes et al. 2019). Its interest is that, by taking the target population as its starting point, it is supposed to be the most likely to meet their needs. Nevertheless, due to its eminently local nature and the limited resources available, this type of logic gives rise to difficulties in disseminating innovations (Surie 2017). Although it allows for the inclusion of beneficiaries, the small scale of this type of logic limits its impact.

Therefore, given their respective strengths and weaknesses, it is common for top-down and bottom-up logics to be mobilized simultaneously and in a complementary manner in the processes by which social innovations are produced. This is particularly visible in national or territorial policies combined with local initiatives dealing with global social problems: mobility, housing, diseases, etc. Nevertheless, this simultaneous mobilization raises several problems, including those of exploiting their complementarities (in terms of populations covered and needs addressed), as well as the tensions that can arise from competition between these logics, in terms of access to resources and to beneficiaries. In short, simultaneous implementation of the different logics of social innovation raises the problem of how it is governed. The remainder of this chapter suggests a solution to these governance issues based on the activity between social entrepreneurs and structures of the social economy. We show in particular that an essential objective of their entrepreneurial activity is to play an intermediation role coordinating the different economic levels: underground, middleground and upperground.

From this perspective, we put forward an original conceptual framework to understand the extent to which entrepreneurs participate in the development of social innovations promoting inclusion. We propose to explore this conceptual framework in the case of mobility among the elderly and disabled in order to better understand how entrepreneurs as intermediaries allow for the development of social innovations, notably because of their cognitive and relational dimension.

7.2. The case of the mobility of vulnerable people in Lorraine

The case study concerns the implementation of an adapted transport system for elderly and vulnerable people with special needs (Laville and Nyssens 2001). After presenting the context of the case, we discuss the results of the investigation: the entrepreneurial process and the role of the actors. We adopted an abductive approach. The researchers collected two types of data. The primary data came from three semi-directive interviews with the director of one of the retirement homes involved in the social innovation, who was also the director of Omnibus Lorraine, the organization that was carrying out the social innovation. Each interview lasted nearly two hours. They were complemented by secondary data (statutes of the association supporting the social innovation in 2008, 2012 and 2014; statutes of the society of collective interest (SCIC in French) in 2014; documentary research on the founding members and on the structure). Conversations with the director allowed us to refine our research results.

This collection was then subjected to an overall analysis and a thematic analysis. The themes selected concerned the levels of the territory (upperground, middleground and underground), the logics of governance (top-down and bottom-up) and the modalities of intermediation (cognitive and relational).

7.2.1. The context of the case

The structure, initially in the form of an association when it was created in 2008, was called "Omnibus 54". It resulted from the merger of two retirement homes, Sainte-Thérèse (Ludres) and Notre-Dame du Bon Repos (Maxéville), both located in the suburbs of Nancy, in the French Grand-Est region, with the major support of the Congregation of the Sisters of Saint-Charles in Nancy. The purpose of this structure was, at that time, to transport elderly people who were being cared for by the daycare services run in the two establishments. The objective was to allow elderly people to take advantage of the daycare places made available to them within the framework of the French Alzheimer's policy.

It should be remembered that such places were created in particular to support family caregivers: they could benefit from a time of recuperation, meeting with other families and medical professionals. These places also allowed elderly people who were still autonomous but, for some of them, isolated at home to take part in nursing home activities, to renew social ties, to be monitored by caregivers and to maintain certain abilities. An induced objective was also to accustom these elderly people to the eventual prospect of one day moving permanently to residences.

Table 7.1 summarizes the history. In 2012, this association saw a change in its target population. The aim was to offer specialized transport to "frail and dependent people (elderly and disabled people, etc.)" and to include the possibility of providing expensive services, with the aim of strengthening the association's financial resources. Two other retirement homes integrated the founding members. The first was Bas-Château supported by the Vincent de Paul foundation: it was created in 1867 by the congregation of the Sisters of Charity of Strasbourg and presents itself as defending a humanist vision in its professional practice. The second was the public interest group "Growing Up and Growing Old in the Colombey area of Southern Toul".

In 2014, "Omnibus 54" became "Omnibus Lorraine". Its activity was changing. It was still transporting the elderly and the disabled, but it mentioned "the elderly, people with disabilities and people on the road to integration". Its target widened and the qualification became more precise. To this was added a new activity: "to ensure a regulatory and administrative intelligence on the mobility of frail and dependent people" (Article 2 of the 2014 statutes). Other retirement homes also joined the project: Les grands jardins and the Aurore home (accommodation for disabled adults).

At the end of 2014, a significant change occurred: the association became an SCIC, which is a specific type of cooperative society characterized by multiple memberships, which may include, within different colleges, beneficiaries, representatives of public authorities and other companies, and employees.

The change in structure is explained by the association's limitations in terms of management and organization of transport. The statutes recalled the genesis of the organization and specified the interest of the, in this case, "mobility problems of physically, cognitively or socially fragile people" (Article 4 of the statutes). Its purpose remained that of building economically sustainable solutions accessible to all. The aims were similar to those found in the social economy, i.e. the pre-eminence of the human being, democracy, solidarity, multiple memberships with the aim of collective interest beyond the individual interests of its members and social, economic and cultural integration in Lorraine.

	Statutes of 10/11/2008	Statutes of 27/02/2012	Statutes of 02/02/2014	Statutes of 02/12/2014
Name	Omnibus 54	Omnibus 54	Omnibus Lorraine	Omnibus Lorraine
Legal structure	Association	Association	Association	SCIC
Main purpose	Pooling resources to offer transportation to elderly people who are cared for by the daycare services run by the two establishments (ex officio members)	Pooling of members' resources (transport in relation to the elderly and disabled and any other activity and/or service contributing to the achievement of its purpose, including onerous services)	– Pooling members' resources for the transportation of frail or dependent persons – Ensuring a regulatory and administrative watch in the field of the elderly and disabled	Proposing and implementing solutions to the mobility problems of physically, cognitively or socially fragile people
Ex officio/ founding members	– Sainte Thérèse de Ludres retirement home – Notre-Dame du Bon Repos de Maxéville retirement home – Congregation of the Sisters of Saint Charles	– Sainte Thérèse retirement home – Notre-Dame du Bon Repos retirement home – Bas-Château retirement home supported by the Vincent de Paul Foundation – The public interest group "Growing Up and Growing Old in the Colombey Area of Southern Toul"	– Sainte Thérèse care home – Notre-Dame du Bon Repos care home – Bas-Château care home – Les grands jardins care home – The Aurora home	Four categories of partners: – associations and foundations who initiated the project (those of the omnibus Lorraine association) – the service's beneficiary structures – voluntary (individuals or legal organizations) – employees (at least one year of seniority)

Table 7.1. *Major changes in the structure of the social innovation*

7.2.2. *The Omnibus entrepreneurial process*

An analysis of the data revealed a specific entrepreneurial process represented as a timeline (Figure 7.2).

Figure 7.2. *Representation of the Omnibus business process*

The starting point (1) was the opening of the daycare centers. The leader then recalled the political context of this opening, which would lead to identification of the need (2), linked to displacement of the targeted persons. He explained[1]:

> Omnibus started with a problem, which we were not able to manage immediately. At the time, I was working in a care home, and we were at a time when what we call daycare centers were opening. The government was implementing with the Alzheimer's policy. [...] The possibility of receiving people during the day and they go home in the evening. [...] The daycare centers opened and then quickly failed fill up. So we had very low occupancy rates. At the beginning we said to ourselves that there was a problem in our area, that we didn't communicate well enough. [...] And very soon after the first daycare centers, the government published a decree [concerning the implementation of adapted transportation]. I think they had identified that in order to go to the daycare center, people had to travel.

Indeed, the target population was specific. Elderly people may have "cognitive problems", some of them have difficulty "arranging transport because they do not have the intellectual means, they forget, they are

---

1 Verbatim translated into English.

confused". It seemed obvious that they "naturally cannot use public services". As a result of the government's decree, resources were allocated to care homes to organize transportation. The government only indicated without specifying the operational organizational modalities that this was up to care homes to organize, with the given transport envelope. It specified that if the care home did not organize transport, it must pay back a part of the resources to the user so that they can organize it. However, it appears obvious that this option did not solve the initial difficulty.

Several actors were trying to meet the need by soliciting operators already in business. However, they all offered an unsatisfactory response (3) because of the population's specifics. Indeed, "it is not enough to take people home"; they have to be accompanied from armchair or sofa to and from the site.

The first operators approached were cabs, but they were not used to transporting elderly people at fixed times. "Then, we will run into the economic problem, because cabs have significant costs." In addition, few took adapted chairs or walking frames. The second type of operator solicited was "the medicalized structures which are ambulances and light medical vehicles". However, they also have high costs and are used to being paid by social security or hospitals. "We have to pay them directly and now we are faced with costs usually covered by social security and we can't take them on." The manager explains that they then turned to a third type of operator: "Small vehicles, individual transport [...] more historical operators, in Nancy in particular we had the GIHP [Group for the Integration of the Physically Disabled] which was identified as the public transport operator for the handicapped."

However, these operators were not often available because this was not their target, and "the cost remained significant despite everything, because financing the elderly is not quite the same as financing the disabled". Finally, for reasons of cost, adaptation of the support and the nature of the target user, the need could not be covered by traditional market operators or by those who worked with state funding. This being said, this search for solutions made it possible to specify the need (4), which went beyond the simple transport of people; the medico-social aspect proved to be very important when people were suffering from Alzheimer's disease and dementia. "You drop the person off in front of their house. You ask them, 'Do you have your key?', 'Yes I do', 'Do you know how to get home?' 'Yes I do'. Then, they take two steps and forget, wander the city and you lose them." The mobility of these people requires that we also think about their installation in a chair, (re-)dress them, put their shoes on them or take them off. "We realized that we really needed the know-how of a medical and social assistant. The manager then explained that these observations led him to decide to provide the transport himself 'since we finally have the skills to support people'."

This is how the idea of creating an association took shape (5), especially since "a partner from another daycare center said: 'If you do that, I'm interested too'". Given the cooperation that was emerging, the manager and this partner saw the importance of specifying "who carries what, who does what". The association took shape. A vehicle and a driver were mobilized. "The driver was, and this is an important point, culturally from a care home; he was accultured to elderly people, to support, he was sensitive to these issues."

The choice was then made to retain a person from the medico-social world who would become a driver, rather than selecting a driver who would become an attendant. The association was growing steadily (6). Other establishments started to join the idea. "The growth is progressive, 36 members in one to two years. Every year, new partners joined the association; the board of directors expanded." To ensure coherence in governance, the board of directors was composed of the association's members. However, the question of the regulatory framework arose (7). Indeed, questions that the actors had not thought of arose.

> Do we have the right to transport these people? They realized that they were operating in a regulated field that is the transportation of persons […]. We were starting to wake up, to ask ourselves questions. This phase of questioning came gradually from the partners with whom the actors were collaborating, because "the competition had spotted us".

This led to: "What is this thing, a non-taxed association, but what is this?" Pressure was beginning to be exerted on the association, especially as it began to work with a structure focused on disability. The traditional transport actors who were collaborating with this structure had been "ejected". Cabs were asking, "What the hell is this? Who are these people? Where do they come from? We've been on the square for 20 years and all of a sudden an association comes along, we don't know what it is, it's weird, and it is taking over the market."

The pressure had no immediate consequences. However, the actors questioned the legal and regulatory framework. The actors then realized the very heavy framework, and said to themselves: "If this had happened before we developed the association, we would not have innovated." The framework was indeed very cumbersome. The difficulties emerged. "Very quickly, we identified a major player, the DREAL[2], an authority in France, which we did not know, because we are not from the sector." The actors decided to contact it, and in good faith, explained what they were doing and their reasons. They looked at the texts that required a degree for this activity, which the leader passed. "I took a training course [...] I gained a diploma, the capacity to transport people."

The association then submitted a file to ask the DREAL for authorization to operate and thus a transport license. The actors were convinced that "things will happen naturally". However, the organization pointed out that the law did not provide for an association to be eligible for a transport license, because "you have to be registered in the trade and company register and, in France, an association cannot be registered in the trade register." A battle with the State's legal services began to register the association in the commercial register, but this proved impossible. The actors then asked themselves: "What are we then? What do we do? Do we continue, do we stop... What's going on?" The DREAL members then proposed an option. The association fell within the framework of private transport, and the users were members of the association, members who were, however, the people transported and not the retirement home. It then became a transport service for the members of the association and the transport diploma was not necessary.

The association then decided to change its legal status (8). However, this was done after many debates which revolved, on the one hand, around the desire to maintain the social innovation essential for vulnerable people to be able to come to daycare and, on the other hand, around the operational management of the proposed option. Indeed, "getting all users to join is complicated, because they change all the time. There are 300 of them, and that means a general meeting with elderly people with Alzheimer's disease. We can't figure out governance." The players sought solutions and discovered another model: the SCIC. Specialists explained to them that they could transform the association into an SCIC: "You keep the history, you

---

2 *Direction Régionale de l'Environnement, de l'Aménagement et du Logement* (French Regional Directorate for the Environment, Planning and Housing). These regional public services are in charge of the regional implementation of national policies for sustainable development.

transfer the funds, the cooperative remains in a spirit close to an association, etc." The general assembly of the association acts on the transformation, which goes hand in hand with taxation. The transport license was also obtained. "We followed the rules and since 2015 we complied with regulations. We had a control in 2019, by the DREAL, which tells us that everything is fine. So, there you go, we're happy."

7.2.3. *Omnibus executives, intermediation players*

The mobility project for the elderly originated from an initiative from the top down (creation of daycare centers within care homes, planned within the framework of the Alzheimer's policy), which followed a top-down logic. The blind spot represented by the transportation of the people concerned was very quickly identified. The solution to the need envisaged by the upperground structures was thus essentially based on the existing offer on the market for the transport of people (cabs and light medical vehicles).

Such recourse to market mechanisms presents two main types drawback that limit its social impact: (1) difficulties in meeting the actual need of the people concerned, which requires not only a home transfer service but also support in the first steps of returning to the home; (2) a cost that is too high given the funding granted. For their part, retirement home executives start from the actual need, observed among the people concerned and their families, following a bottom-up logic. It can therefore be noted that the transport of people is only one stage in a complete medico-social service. Hence, the choice was made to internalize it and to have it managed by professionals from the medico-social field. Nevertheless, such a logic gives rise to a confrontation with the upperground on several levels. First, despite its specificities, the service is part of the institutional framework of the transport of people, totally unknown to the retirement homes at the origin of the project. Second, although it is limited to the beneficiaries of member associations, it competes with passenger transport companies (cab and medical transport companies), which are subject to specific regulations. This tension was amplified when the decision was taken by the project's initiators to extend it to people with mental disabilities, to the detriment of historical actors. Finally, the top-down and bottom-up logics of social innovation, implemented respectively by the upperground (the State) and the underground (retirement home executives), gave rise to different types of inadequacy: in relation to the actual needs of the beneficiaries and in relation to the institutional and regulatory framework. They have generated tensions, resulting in dissatisfaction and even health risks for users of daycare centers and actors of the transportation sector challenging the positive discussion on the grounds of unfair competition.

Entrepreneurial activities aimed at the development and institutionalization of social innovation through the Omnibus Lorraine structure have helped to reduce these tensions. To this end, the organization's leaders have contributed to the development of two types of intermediation processes: a cognitive intermediation process and a relational intermediation process.

The leaders of the different structures involved played a central role in developing shared spaces for different members of the ecosystem, which are cognitive (common knowledge, shared objectives and rationalities), organizational (belonging to a common organization or social group) and physical. This activity of developing shared spaces involved different levels of actors and manifested itself in different forms. A first initiative to develop shared spaces was the organization of meetings where the contours of the transport project were defined. These meetings were held outside any formal framework, bringing together only a small number of partners, retirement home executives who were used to working together. This first circle gradually expanded as the project progressed. Nevertheless, its first concretization, through the purchase of vehicles and mobilization of staff, required a reinforcement of this dynamic through a formalization, in 2008, of the group in an associative form (the Omnibus 54 association), whose board of directors was mainly made up of executives participating in the project. This board of directors provided an opportunity for the project not only to discuss the transport project but also to exchange views on other projects.

The increase in tensions with the upperground linked to the extension of activity towards the transport of mentally disabled people led to the structure's subsequent evolution through the adoption of a cooperative society status in 2014. Apart from the fact that it conveyed a shift of the project towards the upperground by now benefiting from the support and funding of public actors, this legal form constituted an additional step in intermediation between the ecosystem's different levels (underground to upperground). This was particularly visible in the constitution of the four colleges, which allocated an important place to underground and middleground actors: organizations at the origin of the project, medical and social structures that benefit from the project, volunteers and employees.

More marginally, and in line with the work of Burt (1995), the director of the Omnibus acted as a resource broker (Muller and Tanguy 2019). In addition to his involvement in seeking and obtaining funding from the upperground, his action mainly resulted in installing the structure's offices in premises provided by a project partner. It facilitated the circulation of knowledge and resources (Morrison 2008) and, therefore, of creative ideas, thus facilitating their appropriation by the stakeholders of the social innovation. This played an important role in the success of the project: the offices acted as an important shared space for developing communities of practice of employees and managers.

Such places created common spaces for deliberation and negotiation that allowed them to regulate, and even to align, their objectives and rationalities (Berro and Leroux 2010; Amisse et al. 2012). Aware that the project, which was initially conceived from an essentially medico-social perspective, also fell within the field of personal transportation, the Omnibus' leaders played a pivotal role in adapting it to the institutional and regulatory contracts of the upperground: compliance with transport legislation, identification and implementation of the most appropriate legal status (the SCIC), approval by state agencies, etc.

These actions thus allowed acceptance of the project by the actors from the upperground. Through their intermediation, the structure's leaders contributed decisively to developing the innovation. It can nevertheless be noted that they also benefited from favorable initial conditions. The first was the existence of a developed and coherent upperground, having benefited from an important experience in public policies related to old age (Pouchadon and Martin 2018). Second, they had a pre-existing and already coherent middleground relating to accommodation of the dependent elderly that could be exploited and reoriented towards the issue of their mobility.

7.3. Conclusion

Starting from an analysis of the production of social innovations through the lens of the creative territory framework, this chapter highlighted the role played by social entrepreneurs in their development. A processual approach to entrepreneurship allowed us to highlight the fact that their contribution goes beyond their direct involvement in creative processes but also encompasses a role of intermediation between the different actors and levels of the territory, both on a relational and cognitive level. Our study allows us to better perceive the role played by entrepreneurs and contributes in this sense to the enrichment of the literature on territorial dynamics and on social economy organizations. Until now, the literature on this topic has been concentrated on the social entrepreneur as a creative actor (Mumford and Moertl 2003; Dutraive et al. 2018) or as an agent of hybridization between social economy organizations and commercial economy (Glémain and Richez-Battesti 2018), and very little has been published on their role of animating and intermediating the processes of developing social innovations.

Finally, in connection with the notion of social innovation, our contribution also sheds light on a mechanism that allows us to better understand the manner and conditions under which social innovations can be truly inclusive. The logic of governance by intermediation carried by leaders makes it possible not only to answer the real social need of the social groups concerned but also to facilitate the diffusion of these innovations via the mechanisms and actors present within the upperground.

7.4. References

Amisse, S., Leroux, I., Muller, P. (2012). Proximities and logics underlying cluster dynamics: The case of the ornamental horticulture cluster in Maine-et-Loire. *Industry and Innovation*, 19(3), 265–283.

Berro, A. and Leroux, I. (2010). Négociation public/privé et coévolution stratégique dans un biocluster. *M@n@gement*, 13(1), 38.

Burt, R.S. (1995). Le capital social, les trous structuraux et l'entrepreneur. *Revue française de sociologie*, 36(4), 599.

Capdevila, I., Cohendet, P., Simon, L. (2017). From a local community to a global influence. How elBulli restaurant created a new epistemic movement in the world of haute cuisine. *Industry and Innovation*, 25(5), 1–24.

Celle, S. (2019). Les innovations sociales autour du travail dans les entreprises de l'ESS – Un éclairage historique à partir d'études de cas en Picardie. *Marché et organisations*, 36(3), 39–60.

Cohendet, P., Grandadam, D., Simon, L. (2010). The anatomy of the creative city. *Industry and Innovation*, 17(1), 91–111.

Dechamp, G. and Szostak, B. (2016). Organisational creativity and the creative territory: The nature of influence and strategic challenges for organisations. *M@n@gement*, 19(2), 61–88.

Dedehayir, O., Mäkinen, S.J., Ortt, J.R. (2018). Roles during innovation ecosystem genesis: A literature review. *Technological Forecasting and Social Change*, 136, 18–29.

Djellal, F. and Gallouj, F. (2009). Innovation dans les services et entrepreneuriat : au-delà des conceptions industrialistes et technologistes du développement durable. *Innovations*, 29(1), 59.

Dutraive, V., Szostak, B.L., Tiran, A. (2018). Vers la compréhension de l'entrepreneur de demain : s'inspirer de l'entrepreneur dans les industries culturelles et créatives. Working papers, BETA, 2018-49, Strasbourg.

Eynaud, P. and Mourey, D. (2015). Apports et limites de la production du chiffre dans l'entreprise sociale. *Revue française de gestion*, 247(2), 85–100.

Fisher, C.M. and Amabile, T.M. (2011). Creativity, improvisation and organizations. In *The Routledge Companion to Creativity*, Rickards, T., Runco, M.A., Moger, S. (eds). Routledge, New York.

Gartner, W.B. (1985). A conceptual framework for describing the phenomenon of new venture creation. *The Academy of Management Review*, 10(4), 696–706.

Gartner, W.B. (1988). Who is an entrepreneur? Is the wrong question. *American Journal of Small Business*, 12(4), 11–32.

Glémain, P. and Richez-Battesti, N. (2018). De l'économie sociale et solidaire à l'entreprise sociale : entre tournant entrepreneurial et innovation. Une clé de lecture. *Marché et organisations*, 31(1), 13–19.

Grandadam, D., Cohendet, P., Simon, L. (2013). Places, spaces and the dynamics of creativity: The video game industry in Montreal. *Regional Studies*, 47(10), 1701–1714.

Gupta, A.K., Sinha, R., Koradia, D., Patel, R., Parmar, M., Rohit, P., Patel, H. (2003). Mobilizing grassroots' technological innovations and traditional knowledge, values and institutions: Articulating social and ethical capital. *Futures*, 35(9), 975–987.

Héraud, J.A. and Muller, Z. (2017). Creativity management: Causation, effectuation and will. In *The Global Management of Creativity*, Wagner, M., Valls-Pasola, J., Burger-Helmchen, T. (eds). Routledge, New York.

Hjorth, D. (2017). Critique nouvelle – An essay on affirmative-performative entrepreneurship research. *Revue de l'entrepreneuriat*, 16(1), 47–54.

Hjorth, D., Strati, A., Drakopoulou, S.D., Weik, E. (2018). Organizational creativity, play and entrepreneurship: Introduction and framing. *Organization Studies*, 39(2/3), 155–168.

Howells, J. (2006). Intermediation and the role of intermediaries in innovation. *Research Policy*, 35(5), 715–728.

Kirzner, I.M. (2009). The alert and creative entrepreneur: A clarification. *Small Business Economics*, 32(2), 145–152.

Klein, J.L., Boucher, J., Camus, A., Noiseux, Y., Champagne, C. (2019). *Trajectoires d'innovation : des émergences à la reconnaissance. Innovation sociale*. Presses de l'Université du Québec.

Lamine, W., Jack, S., Fayolle, A., Chabaud, D. (2015). One step beyond? Towards a process view of social networks in entrepreneurship. *Entrepreneurship and Regional Development*, 27(7/8), 413–429.

Langley, A., Smallman, C., Tsoukas, H., Van de Ven, A.H. (2013). Process studies of change in organization and management: Unveiling temporality, activity, and flow. *Academy of Management Journal*, 56(1), 1–13.

Laville, J.L. and Nyssens, M. (2001). *Les services sociaux entre associations, marché et État : l'aide aux personnes âgées*. La Découverte, Paris.

Le Velly, R. (2008). La détermination du prix équitable. *Gestion*, 33(1), 59–65.

Lethielleux, L. and Paturel, D. (2017). Innovation sociale et travail social. *Forum*, 150(1), 7–15.

March, J.G. (1991). Exploration and exploitation in organizational learning. *Organization Science*, 2(1), 71–87.

Mehouachi, C., Grandadam, D., Cohendet, P., Simon, L. (2017). Creative capabilities and the regenerative power of creative industries: Local and global ingredients. In *The Global Management of Creativity*, Wagner, M., Valls-Pasola, J., Burger-Helmchen, T. (eds). Routledge, New York.

Morrison, A. (2008). Gatekeepers of knowledge within industrial districts: Who they are, how they interact. *Regional Studies*, 42(6), 817–835.

Moulaert, F. (2009). Social innovation: Institutionally embedded, territorialy (re)produced. In *Social Innovation and Territorial Development*, Maccallum, D., Moulaert, F., Hillier, J., Vicari Haddock, S. (eds). Ashgate, Farnham.

Moulaert, F. and Sekia, F. (2003). Territorial innovation models: A critical survey. *Regional Studies*, 37(3), 289–302.

Muller, P. (2021). La production des innovations sociales : une analyse par le modèle de l'écologie créative. *Technologie et Innovation*, 21(6), 1–12.

Muller, P. and Tanguy, C. (2019). Les organisations de l'économie sociale et solidaire (ESS) comme intermédiaires de l'innovation sociale : leurs apports... et limites. *Innovations*, 58(1), 189–217.

Muller, P., Szostak, B.L., Burger-Helmchen, T. (2020). Le rôle d'intermédiation des activités entrepreneuriales du middleground dans la circulation des idées créatives. Le cas du Krautrock. *Revue internationale P.M.E.*, 33(3/4), 139–168.

Mumford, M.D. and Moertl, P. (2003). Cases of social innovation: Lessons from two innovations in the 20th century. *Creativity Research Journal*, 15(2/3), 261–266.

Nambisan, S. and Baron, R.A. (2013). Entrepreneurship in innovation ecosystems: Entrepreneurs' self-regulatory processes and their implications for new venture success. *Entrepreneurship Theory and Practice*, 37(5), 1071–1097.

Pouchadon, M.L. and Martin, P. (2018). Politiques de la vieillesse, politiques de l'autonomie : quelles dynamiques territoriales et démocratiques ? *Retraite et société*, 79(1), 83–103.

Raedersdorf, S. (2018). La construction d'un outil de contrôle de gestion innovant dans l'économie sociale et solidaire : le cas de la fondation Apprentis d'Auteuil. *Innovations*, 57(3), 109–136.

Richez-Battesti, N. and Vallade, D. (2009). Économie sociale et solidaire et innovation sociale : premières observations sur un incubateur dédié en Languedoc Roussillon. *Innovations*, 30(2), 41.

Richez-Battesti, N., Petrella, F., Vallade, D. (2012). L'innovation sociale, une notion aux usages pluriels : quels enjeux et défis pour l'analyse ? *Innovations*, 38(2), 15.

Saebi, T., Foss, N.J., Linder, S. (2019). Social entrepreneurship research: Past achievements and future promises. *Journal of Management*, 45(1), 70–95.

Sarasvathy, S.D., Dew, N., Read, S., Wiltbank, R. (2008). Designing organizations that design environments: Lessons from entrepreneurial expertise. *Organization Studies*, 29(3), 331–350.

Sarazin, B., Cohendet, P., Simon, L. (2017). *Les communautés d'innovation : de la liberté créatrice à l'innovation organisée. Regards sur la pratique*. EMS, Caen.

Seyfang, G. and Smith, A. (2007). Grassroots innovations for sustainable development: Towards a new research and policy agenda. *Environmental Politics*, 16(4), 584–603.

Simon, L. (2009). Underground, upperground et middle-ground : les collectifs créatifs et la capacité créative de la ville. *Management International*, 13, 37–51.

Stolarick, K. and Florida, R. (2006). Creativity, connections and innovation: A study of linkages in the Montréal region. *Environment and Planning*, 38(10), 1799–1817.

Surie, G. (2017). Creating the innovation ecosystem for renewable energy via social entrepreneurship: Insights from India. *Technological Forecasting and Social Change*, 121, 184–195.

Swedberg, R. (2006). The cultural entrepreneur and the creative industries: Beginning in Vienna. *Journal of Cultural Economics*, 30(4), 243–261.

Swyngedouw, E. (2005). Governance innovation and the citizen: The Janus face of governance-beyond-the-State. *Urban Studies*, 42(11), 1991–2006.

Tracey, P. and Stott, N. (2017). Social innovation: A window on alternative ways of organizing and innovating. *Innovation*, 19(1), 51–60.

Younes, D., Jacob, M.R., Marti, I. (2019). L'innovation sociale sur les territoires – Comment passer de l'intervention exogène à la communauté innovante ? *Revue française de gestion*, 45(280), 75–90.

Zahra, S.A. and Nambisan, S. (2012). Entrepreneurship and strategic thinking in business ecosystems. *Business Horizons*, 55(3), 219–229.

8

Emergence and Diffusion of Diversity Management in Companies Linking a Territory: The Case of the Hérault Region in France

In October 2014, through the so-called CSR Directive 2014/95/EU, the European Union made it mandatory for companies with more than 500 employees and 40 million in turnover to publish non-financial information. The title of the directive explicitly mentions diversity-related information as an important part of this extra-financial publication[1]. This initiative is a recent institutional recognition of the close link between diversity management and corporate social responsibility (CSR) understood as a trend in the evolution of social attitudes towards the responsibilities of companies regarding the societies in which they operate.

More than ever before, companies are required to explicitly report on all aspects of their performance, not only their financial results, but also their environmental and social results, as part of a more comprehensive approach to their performance.

Chapter written by Amel BEN RHOUMA and Elena MASCOVA.

1 Directive 2014/95/EU of the European Parliament and of the Council of October 22, 2014, amending Directive 2013/34/EU as regards disclosure of non-financial and diversity information by some large businesses and certain groups. The text specifies that the European companies concerned must include in the corporate governance statement a description of their diversity policy (objectives, implementation methods and results).

The issue of diversity is one of the main levers of action for CSR within a company, as stated in most of the major national international texts on CSR. The sixth principle of the United Nations Global Compact stipulates that member organizations must contribute to the elimination of all discrimination in employment and professional life. In France, the public authorities have put in place various measures to encourage companies to act on diversity since the publication in 2004 of the Claude Bébéar report (2004). In 2007, the French Agency for Diversity Managers (*Agence française des managers de la diversité* (AFMD)) was created with the objective of developing operational tools to support employers in promoting diversity. In 2013, the regional section of the AFMD/LH2 barometer Perception of the Equal Opportunity Climate by Managers of SMEs (Île-de-France and Aquitaine) showed the existence of territorial disparities in the consideration of different diversity issues and in the development of actions dedicated to their management.

The AFMD, with the financial support of the French National Agency for Social Cohesion and Equal Opportunities (*Agence nationale pour la cohésion sociale et l'égalité des chances* (AcSé)), has launched an action aimed at continuing the process of promoting diversity management on the ground. This action places at the heart of its reflections the co-construction and sharing of competences in terms of diversity management between local actors (between companies, public authorities, those involved in employment, training and integration, associations, etc.). The action was launched in 2015, and the Hérault department was selected as the relevant territory to conduct this project.

We contributed to carrying the project out. This chapter explains the current state of the diffusion and operationalization of diversity management and the context of its emergence in the Hérault department. The results presented in this chapter are therefore based on the analysis of interviews and workshop reports with representatives of local organizations that are members of the FACE Hérault club, as well as a survey that was disseminated on a wider scale.

The objective of our research was to understand the influence of the institutional environment on the emergence, diffusion and appropriation of diversity management by organizations operating within the Hérault department. To do this, we mobilized the sociological approach of neo-institutional theory (Meyer and Rowan 1977; Dimaggio and Powell

1983; Scott 1995), which is at the origin of the notion of an institutional environment.

We relied on the concepts of institutional entrepreneurship and institutional isomorphism proposed by sociological neo-institutionalism. The first concept helped us to analyze the process of institutional change that led to the emergence of diversity at the scale of the territory (assimilated here to an organizational field). As for isomorphism, it helped us to identify the factors and pressures determining the diffusion and operationalization of diversity management by organizations operating at the local level. Section 8.1 develops the theoretical basis of our research. Section 8.2 discusses the details of our methodology for conducting quantitative and qualitative research and studies of diversity management in organizations in the Hérault department. Section 8.3 presents our results and discussion of the emergence, diffusion and operationalization of diversity at the territorial level before concluding.

8.1. The emergence and diffusion of diversity management between isomorphism and institutional entrepreneurship

Demographic diversity (or heterogeneity) refers to the degree to which a unit (such as a leadership team, a work team or an organization) is heterogeneous with respect to demographic characteristics: age, gender, nationality, seniority, functional area of training and family status (Pelled et al. 1999). The concept of "diversity" originated in the United States in the 1960s and 1970s, when women and ethnic minorities were given preferential treatment to rebalance their representation in qualified jobs within the framework of the federal affirmative action (AA) policy. Diversity management as a new managerial approach appeared in the 1990s in response to the exhaustion of these policies. Kelly and Dobbin (1998) show how equal employment opportunity affirmative action (EEO-AA) specialists recruited by American companies gradually became "diversity managers" and contributed to the construction and dissemination of diversity management. The aim of diversity management is to change attitudes to eliminate any discriminatory behavior and establish a culture of tolerance that allows for the inclusion of everyone with their contributions and differences.

In France, diversity management emerged much later than in the United States, in the mid-2000s. French companies seized on the American concept of "diversity" to appropriate the legal framework for the fight against discrimination and equal opportunity, which has been constantly evolving since the principle of equality was established in the French constitution in October 1958, and which was finalized in 2001 with the law on the fight against discrimination[2]. Diversity proposes to consider all differences as assets for both individuals and companies, thus contributing to their performance and competitiveness. Diversity management is becoming a necessity, with proactive strategies in favor of minorities, the adoption of a positive vocabulary and a managerial approach, the creation of charters and guides, the creation of the job of diversity manager in certain companies and the creation of a professional association in this field.

Diversity could thus be likened to an informal institution, i.e. to sets of values and beliefs anchored at different levels, in particular at the organizational and societal levels. Informal institutions owe their appearance to neo-institutional theory (NIT). Neo-institutionalism is a school of thought that developed in the late 19th and early 20th centuries in the United States. It supports the role of institutions in shaping agents' preferences and choices. It is based on formal institutions (such as the family, the firm, the market, etc.). NIT is a multidisciplinary approach to organizations. Beyond the commonly accepted purpose of the organization, i.e. coordination in order to accomplish certain tasks, it seems that the organization is characterized by modalities of appearance, of development, of relations in its field that should be explored, such as the appearance and diffusion of diversity management practices.

There are two approaches to NIT: an economic one and a sociological one, both of which have been appropriated by the management sciences. While the economic approach mobilizes different concepts, such as Simon's (1956) limited rationality, to explain the existence of the firm, the sociological approach considers organizations to be a function of their

---

2 This law covers all fields of professional activity, defines the notions of direct and indirect discrimination, sets out a set of 16 criteria for discrimination and provides for the reversal of evidence, as well as the sentences envisaged: €45,000 for an individual, €225,000 for a legal person and up to three years' imprisonment.

environment. Sociological neo-institutionalism develops theories of an institutional environment in addition to the technical environment (Meyer and Rowan 1977). The institutional environment would be made up of myths, ceremonies and beliefs to which organizations must adapt, as in the case of beliefs about diversity management. The reflection on the institutional environment of organizations initiated by Meyer and Rowan (1977) was continued by DiMaggio and Powell (1983) to answer the question of why organizations are similar.

To this end, DiMaggio and Powell borrow the notion of a "field" from Pierre Bourdieu and refer to it as the level of analysis for NIT. They define "the organizational field" as an arena in which mutually recognizing organizations that share the same sense of reality and cognitive patterns interact around institutionalized practices and forms (DiMaggio and Powell 1983). In each organizational field (e.g. the territory of location), the quest for legitimacy and the nature of the pressures in the institutional environment result in the propensity of organizations to resemble each other. This homogeneity is the product of a process of institutional isomorphism. DiMaggio and Powell (1983) identify three forms of isomorphism. There is a coercive form resulting from formal and informal pressures (laws, requirements/expectations of clients, etc.) from organizations in the field and pressures resulting from the cultural expectations of a society, often forcing actors to innovate (ecological expectations, for example). The second form of isomorphism is called normative and places importance on the phenomenon of professionalization (uniformity, reproduction, socialization). Professionalization can result from formal educational devices or from the growth of professional networks, which are channels for disseminating organizational models such as those that can be formed at the territorial level. The third form of isomorphism is mimicry, which tends to develop in situations of uncertainty, pushing organizations to adopt solutions known and practiced by other organizations in the field. Legitimacy is enhanced by the stability derived from these arrangements and promotes access to resources (Pfeffer and Salancik 1978; Deephouse et al. 2017).

Beyond the concept of isomorphism, NIT has undergone, since the 1990s, a major turn that has constantly given it strategic accents by including agency (DiMaggio 1988) in order to explain institutional change (rather than continuity and stability) and the role of the actor as an agent of change rather than a mere relay and bearer of institutions. The authors of the NIT have thus developed the idea that organizations are subject to cultural and cognitive pressures from many actors in the environment. The integration of agency into NIT to provide it with an internal tool for explaining institutional change has given rise to a new concept in this theory, that of institutional entrepreneurship. This concept, introduced by DiMaggio (1988), is the embodiment of the actor's role as an agent of institutional change. It refers to actors with resources and power who act to change institutions in their favor.

The concept of institutional entrepreneurship is based on an agency of a projective nature (Emirbayer and Mische 1998). Thus, leaders act intentionally to achieve an institutional change project that they have predefined. For this reason, it seems to us to be suitable for analyzing the emergence of diversity and the management of diversity on the scale of a territory, such as the department of Hérault. Indeed, before spreading, informal institutions like diversity must first emerge. This emergence depends on the role of actors and organizations in the processes of institutional change. New institutions emerge when organized actors with sufficient resources (institutional business leaders) see in them an opportunity to realize interests they value highly (DiMaggio 1988).

Battilana et al. (2009) consider institutional business leaders (organizations or individuals) as agents who initiate and actively participate in implementing changes that diverge from existing institutions, regardless of whether the initial intention was to change the institutional environment and without knowing whether the changes will be successfully implemented. Such changes could be initiated within the confines of an organization or in a broader institutional context, within which the action is embedded, such as the case of a territory. Greenwood and Suddaby (2006) show that divergent changes were initiated by organizations with high status and supposedly at the center of an organizational field. The status of the organization in which an individual actor is embedded, as well as their position in the hierarchy and position in the informal network within an organization, are likely to influence not only independently, but also jointly, the likelihood that a particular actor will engage in entrepreneurship (Battilana 2006). Battilana et al. (2009) propose a model of the institutional entrepreneurship process in different phases ranging from the emergence of institutional entrepreneurship to their implementation of change. The main steps in this process are:

establishment of divergent change, creation of a vision for a different change and mobilization of allies to implement the change.

NIT and its two complementary concepts of institutional entrepreneurship and isomorphism seem to us to be suitable for the respective analysis of the emergence and diffusion of diversity within organizations located in the Hérault department in France. In addition, our theoretical framework encompasses the main approaches to diversity management from the existing literature. For example, Thomas and Ely (1996) explain the commitment to diversity by the desire to match internal employee demographics with those of customers and the market served, which amounts to a strategic and utilitarian approach for organizations.

Diversity management could also oscillate between ethical or philanthropic approaches, on the one hand, and a utilitarian approach, on the other hand. Indeed, in Great Britain, Kirton et al. (2007, p. 1992) emphasize the "position of tension" in which diversity officers find themselves: on the one hand, their professional mandate consists of carrying the business case for diversity, to which many of them sincerely adhere; on the other hand, these managers generally have a broader personal vision of organizational transformation, including a social justice objective.

Our empirical study on the emergence and diffusion of diversity management practices within organizations located in the Hérault department includes small- and medium-sized enterprises (SMEs). This type of company has been little explored in the existing literature, which focuses on studying the practices of large companies on a national scale (Bogaert and Vloeberghs 2005; Sippola and Smale 2007; Süß and Kleiner 2008; Klarsfeld 2009; Lauring 2013), neglecting small- and medium-sized companies, which nonetheless play a part in this movement (Berger-Douce 2010).

8.2. Methodological design of the action research

The data analyzed and discussed in this chapter were produced during an action research project conducted in 2015 by the French Diversity Managers Association (*Association française des managers de la diversité* (AFMD))[3].

---

3 The AFMD was created in 2007 at the initiative of several large companies located in France to promote diversity management in companies by providing employers with a set of operational management tools.

The project received financial support from the AcSé. In order to fall within the scope of missions that could be financed by the agency, it had to contribute to the "approach to promoting diversity management in the territories". In order to meet the "territoriality" criterion, the AFMD chose the Hérault department to deploy the action because of its relations with a number of local actors, such as the Hérault departmental (and general) council and Montpellier Business School. The proposed research-action project was to understand the challenges of diversity management as perceived by employers in the Hérault region, to list practices actually developed within companies and to identify the territorial drivers of the diversity promotion approach. In order to arouse the interest and mobilization of local actors, implementation of the project required the construction of multiple legitimacies (Chemla et al. 2017): legitimacy in terms of recognition of the usefulness of the actors and the territory by the actors themselves, academic legitimacy through the participation of researchers and institutional legitimacy through the recognition of the AFMD's role in developing diversity in this territory.

The proposed research design was to be part of this process. It had three components:

– Three focus groups organized with employers in the Hérault region under the auspices of the 1,000 Companies for Equality: Assessment and Progress in Equal Treatment and Diversity meeting cycle. They mobilized about 15 participants from February to April 2015. The participating organizations were recruited through the project's partners' networks, such as the FACE Hérault Foundation and the general council.

– A qualitative study that consisted of a series of semi-structured interviews conducted between February and April 2015 with people in charge of diversity projects within 15 member organizations of the FACE Hérault club[4] (Table 8.1).

– A quantitative survey presented as a barometer and entitled "Concerns and Diversity Management Policies in the Department of Hérault".

---

4 An informal network of employers grouped around the local branch of the Foundation Acting Against Exclusion (*Fondation Agir Contre l'Exclusion* (FACE)), dedicated to discussing the concerns of local companies in terms of their social responsibility.

	Workforce	Main activity	Role of interviewees
A	15	Language service	Quality and CSR manager
B	450	Large-scale distribution	Recruitment officer
C	500	Water, development and environment	HR director
D	730	Social protection	HR development manager
E	150	Organization professional	Quality and CSR manager
F	480	Health	General manager
G	1,000	Computer science	Operational manager
H	5	Energy	Administrative manager
I	140	Social protection	HR manager
J	149	Energy	HR manager and diversity referent
K	460	Communication	Delegate for regional development and disability reference
L	30	Association	General delegate
M	17	HR services	Manager
N	4,200	Transport	Head of jobs and skills
O	-	FACE Hérault club	Former general manager of FACE Hérault

Table 8.1. *List of organizations interviewed*

All the semi-structured interviews, which lasted between one and two hours, were recorded and transcribed. Some of the interviews conducted with actors who participated in the genesis of diversity at the departmental level, such as the interview with the former director of FACE Hérault, were coded by hand to identify and analyze the context, actors and stages regarding the emergence of diversity management at the territorial level. Subsequently, all the transcribed interviews were coded with the qualitative data processing and analysis software NVIVO 11. Coding consists of breaking down a text into units of analysis or units of meaning (words or segments) and then conducting a qualitative or quantitative study of these units. It is a process of de-structuring and then restructuring, with a decontextualization and then a recontextualization (Tesch 1990). The analytical grid used to code the interviews included six major themes, known as nodes in NVIVO: "Determinants of the implementation of a diversity approach", "Formalization of actions in favor of diversity" and "Dimensions of diversity dealt with by the organization". The software allowed for a hierarchical ranking of the nodes of the diversity process. Since the software allowed for a hierarchy of nodes, each main node was then broken down into sub-nodes. Thus, the node "Determinants of the implementation of a diversity approach" was broken down into six "sub-nodes" corresponding to the three forms of isomorphism (coercive, normative and mimetic), to which we added the different approaches to diversity management identified in our literature review, namely the philanthropic approach, the utilitarian approach and the manager's wishes.

The objective of the quantitative survey was to verify the general character of the results obtained during the workshops and interviews. The questionnaire administered via the Monkeysurvey platform consisted of 25 questions and yielded a total of 102 responses. According to the profile of the respondents, 66% belonged to private companies and 20% to associations. Public institutions represented only 5% of the panel respondents. The organizations were of all sizes, with a significant proportion of organizations with less than 50 employees (41%), which was consistent with the economic structure of the territory. According to the 2007 INSEE survey, 96.6% of establishments in the Languedoc–Roussillon region had fewer than 50 employees and only 3.4% had more than 50 employees. The activities of the organizations to which the respondents belonged covered all scales: municipal (4%), departmental (19%), regional (24%), national (21%) and international (27%). The respondents included company directors, HR professionals and managers.

8.3. Results, analysis and discussion

In this section, we present our results and then put them into perspective in the discussion.

8.3.1. *The emergence of diversity management in Hérault: An institutional entrepreneurship model*

The creation of an office of FACE in the Hérault department in 2002, at the initiative of the general council, in order to involve companies in the fight against exclusion could be considered an example of institutional entrepreneurship. Indeed, previously, the institutionalized model for acting against exclusion at the departmental level was based on a certain number of public policies to which companies were not necessarily associated:

> During the constitutive general assembly, there were five companies and a very motivated general council, it was Jean Gatel who implemented a certain number of public policies, and it was Marc Bessière, director of economic development and employment, who led the project and called on the FACE foundation to set up an office in the Hérault. We had a president, from the diversity initiative, head of a company based in a free zone, Khaled Zourray, who was a figure, let's say, of the success of the Republic. And then we started like that. (Interview O., former executive director of FACE Hérault)

By implementing a change that diverged from the institutionalized model to organize the fight against exclusion and involve businesses within the department, the representatives of the Hérault general council at the time effectively acted as institutional business leaders. They were able to identify specific intervention strategies and levers for action to change the existing institutional model around the fight against discrimination and thus play a role in the process of institutional change that should lead to the emergence of diversity at the territorial level. Thus, the launch by the general council of Hérault of a project to create a branch of FACE at a departmental scale and its active participation in making this creation project a reality made it an actor of change.

The high positions of the individual actors, in the personality of Jean Gatel, vice-president of the general council, and that of Marc Bessière, director of the economic division, as well as the high status of their organization, favored initiation of this divergent change in the way that issues related to exclusion are dealt with at the territorial level. This is confirmed by the testimony of FACE Hérault's first executive director, who stated that:

> the initial idea in 2001 was to say that the company has a place in issues related to exclusion, i.e. the question of poverty, mediation, etc. At the time, the question of discrimination did not arise, it was more a question of how to involve the company in employment, education and social policies. It was the

historical FACE with employment, school and mediation. The first ingredient was the general council.

Beyond the social position of the actors, the terrain was relatively homogeneous and conducive to the initiative's development. Indeed, the strong network culture, as well as the frequency of meetings for discussions and exchanges between companies within the department, allowed the economic actors to be mobilized around this new project in favor of the fight against exclusion, which would later become a project in favor of the promotion of diversity management:

> In the Hérault, there are networks for everything. There was the CJD [*Centre des jeunes dirigeants* (Center for Young Managers)], which was very active, and a JCE [*Jeune chambre économique* (Economic Youth Chamber)], which was also very active. I got closer to these networks, and I had access to a whole breeding ground of young and dynamic business leaders who wanted to do different things. (Interview O., former executive director of FACE Hérault)

Our analysis of interviews with the founding actors of FACE Hérault shows that the project's development around the promotion of diversity on the scale of the Hérault department followed the different stages of the process of setting up divergent changes proposed by Battilana et al. (2009). Indeed, before its dissemination to organizations in the territory, diversity management emerged through a process of institutional change that the concept of the NIT business leader allowed us to identify and understand. The creation of a FACE branch in the Hérault department allowed us to create a vision and theorize the institutional project in a way that resonates with the interests, values and problems of potential allies (Boxenbaum 2006). Thus, to develop a vision that frames its project for change, the first FACE club director adopted a form of motivational framing involving the compelling reasons for supporting the project. In addition, to mobilize businesses, she used rhetoric that linked the FACE club project to familiar models, such as the center for young managers, while emphasizing the need for change. These rhetorical strategies link the innovations of institutional stakeholders to familiar models, while emphasizing the need for change (Battilana et al. 2009):

So, I presented it as a new network of companies that was going to carry out a number of actions, notably following the example of what the center for young managers was doing with their "an economy to serve humankind" training. I told them: "It's great what the center is doing, because we're going to train you on these concepts, but come on, we'll do something concrete. That's how it started". (Interview, O.)

The first director of FACE Hérault did not hesitate to define and redefine her institutional project to attract businesses and create a sustainable coalition. In particular, she focused on the flaws of existing institutionalized practices by pointing out that the Center for Young Managers project lacked concreteness and by demonstrating that adopting the proposed vision would fill this gap and ensure improvement. Institutional business leaders often use analogies to legitimize their vision for change (Suddaby and Greenwood 2005). The support of the general council was very helpful to the FACE club in mobilizing the territory's economic actors:

The third interesting ingredient is that we had the state services who were also interested in our success. All this meant that, by the end of the second year, we had 60–70 members with 7 or 8 actions. Very quickly, it grew. (Interview O.)

Formal authorities can help institutional business leaders legalize divergent ideas (Maguire et al. 2004), frame stories and promote recognition and "consumption" of their discourse by other actors. Beyond the emergence of diversity at the scale of the territory, our study seeks to understand how diversity is diffused and operationalized by organizations operating at the local level, a point that we will attempt to shed light on through the analysis of interviews conducted with representatives of these organizations and the various focus groups, as well as the barometer distributed to a larger sample.

8.3.2. Dissemination of diversity management in organizations in the Hérault region: Between normative isomorphism, utilitarianism and the will of the manager

After coding interviews with the organizations involved at the departmental level using NVIVO 11, we established a hierarchical diagram showing the number of interviews mentioning each type of determinant and the total number of references to the determinant (Table 8.2).

	Total number of interviews coded	Total number of encoding references
Nodes\grid\determinants	12	71
Nodes\grid\determinants\det-coercive	6	7
Nodes\grid\determinants\det-mimetic	3	3
Nodes\grid\determinants\det-normative	6	21
Nodes\grid\determinants\det-philanthropic	2	4
Nodes\grid\determinants\det-utilitarian	10	20
Nodes\grid\determinants\det-leadership desire	6	12

Table 8.2. *Determinants of diversity management in the Hérault*

Table 8.2 shows that the number of interviews (encoded elements) that mentioned the determinants was 12 and that 10 out of 12 mentioned the utilitarian approach (20 times) as a determinant of their company's commitment to diversity. Thus, one interviewee states:

> We obviously have in this area [diversity], as in others, a useful and utilitarian approach... Diversity as the "only salvation for the poor" is widely exploited for internal marketing purposes. (Diversity manager, parapublic agency)

Continuing on, two other interviewees from private companies confided:

> Yes, it's related to image. We work a lot with companies, and we want to share this type of commitment. And we have also noticed that large companies who are our clients have come to us for advice on how to implement certain things. It's a source of pride to do things well and to set an example. So, the image issue goes without saying. There is also a desire to resemble the markets in which we would like to go. When you go to the

Spanish market, the Italian market, the Middle East market, Africa, you are in markets that are diverse in any case, and you need diversity to be able to manage that (Operational manager, large international group).

Such a result is consistent with the second paradigm, "access and legitimacy", proposed by Thomas and Ely (1996) to explain American companies' commitment to diversity management policies.

Table 8.2 also shows that 6 out of 12 interviews mentioned the leader's will and coercive and normative isomorphism as determinants. The latter had the highest number of references (21). Indeed, the networking culture that characterizes the Hérault department seems to play an important role in companies' commitment to diversity. The actions and tools proposed at the local level have enabled companies to formalize their diversity management approach. Moreover, the presence of FACE Hérault has above all motivated them to move towards diversity management and the equal treatment plan, which has made it possible to develop tools to implement them. Some of the people we spoke to were "proud" to tell us that "local development enthusiasts" were at the origin of disseminating diversity management and that these practices seemed to be an innovative way of acting that found favor with actors. Today, these same actors seem to be increasingly forced to integrate social criteria, including diversity, in response to legal obligations or at the request of their financiers and clients.

Finally, our results show that, in some companies, especially very small companies, diversity management is above all determined by the management's will, as illustrated by the words of one of our interviewees: "It was already important for the general manager, so it started with him."

The results of our qualitative analysis are in line with those of the quantitative survey carried out among a panel of 100 employers, since legal constraints, integration into thematic networks and society's expectations were the three external determinants of commitment most cited by respondents in terms of diversity management. However, the examples of actions implemented and the dimensions managed underline the need to respond to coercive constraints around diversity, which are constantly increasing at the European and French national scales.

8.3.3. *Operationalizing diversity management: A response to a coercive isomorphism*

In this section, the aim is to draw up a picture of the actions implemented by employers based on the results of the quantitative part of our study, as well as on the interviews. Diversity was an important subject within the organizations in our panel but far from being considered a priority. Thus, 57% of respondents declared that diversity management was an important element but not a priority, and for 21% of respondents, it was a priority element. Of the 68 respondents to the online questionnaire, 62% formalized their commitment to diversity via one of these three tools: charter for professional equality between women and men, diversity charter and the diversity label. Out of 68 respondents, only 22% said they had a position or department specific to diversity management within their organization. Moreover, we found them mainly represented among organizations that had formalized their commitment. This position or service had existed for two to five years for 36% of respondents and less than two years for 18%.

Moreover, 16% declared that they allocated a specific budget to diversity management. However, the absence of a formal commitment among 38% of respondents does not mean that organizations are not investing in the subject, since the majority of these same organizations declared that they had implemented actions related to diversity management. In terms of the actions that organizations implemented, we noted application of collective agreements (55%), integration into HR processes (50%), implementation of measures to promote flexibility in working hours (49%), training and awareness of stereotypes (43%) and integration of diversity management into the organizational culture (43%).

What dimensions of diversity are most invested in? At the top of the list is disability (63%), followed by gender equality (59%) and work/life balance (53%). The least invested in are religion (4%) and sexual orientation (0.68%). It should be noted that the first two dimensions are precisely those for which legal obligations are stronger. In fact, in terms of disability, employers in France with more than 20 employees are subject to the obligation to employ disabled workers. In terms of gender equality, companies with more than 50 employees must produce an agreement on the subject, as well as draw up a report on the comparative situation of the general conditions of employment and training for women and men. There is a tendency for obligations to converge between private and public employers, which shows the importance of coercive isomorphism when it comes to implementing an action related to diversity management. On the other hand, only 14% of the 56 respondents stated that they had put in place systems to effectively measure the impact of diversity management within their organizations.

The in-depth interviews we conducted with representatives of organizations in the territory allowed us to deepen the results of the barometer. Indeed, there are differences between establishments belonging to large groups and organizations with a mainly local presence. For the first type of organization, it is above all a matter of deploying policies designed at the corporate level, leaving local actors little room for maneuver in choosing actions. In return, they have significant resources to implement them and can therefore play the role of sponsors. The latter act within a more flexible framework to implement their vision of diversity management. These organizations, often smaller in size, have a repertoire of actions that promote the values of proximity to target groups (people with disabilities, young people from disadvantaged areas, ethnic minorities, etc.). These actions, which often reflect the manager's vision, are an opportunity to show that the company is firmly rooted in its territory and are supposed to be a sign of a socially responsible company.

8.4. Conclusion

The contribution presented in this chapter tried to explain the emergence and diffusion in a given territory of a very particular type of norm, namely diversity management. The authors' participation in a research-action carried out by a professional association in the field of diversity in the department of Hérault made it possible to produce very rich empirical material based on the qualitative and quantitative aspects of the project. The concepts of institutional entrepreneurship and institutional isomorphisms proposed by sociological neo-institutionalism proved to be particularly powerful explanatory tools. The first concept helped us to analyze the process of institutional change that led to the emergence of diversity at the department level (assimilated here to an organizational field).

As for isomorphism, it helped us to identify the factors and pressures that determine the diffusion and operationalization of diversity management by organizations operating at the local level. Our results show that the emergence of diversity management in the Hérault region of France has followed the stages of the institutional entrepreneurship process proposed by Battilana et al. (2009). The people interviewed insisted on the aspect of professionalization that results from normative isomorphism and on the ethical basis of their organizations' commitment and their own mobilization even though they were aware of utilitarianism and the rise of coercive constraint as a determinant of their organizations' commitment to certain dimensions of diversity. Analysis of the data from our quantitative survey clearly showed coercive isomorphism as the major determinant of the implementation of diversity management by organizations in the Hérault department.

8.5. References

Battilana, J. (2006). Agency and institutions: The enabling role of individuals' social position. *Organization*, 13(5), 653–676.

Battilana, J., Leca, B., Boxenbaum, E. (2009). How actors change institutions: Towards a theory of institutional entrepreneurship. *Academy of Management Annals*, 3(1), 65–107.

Bébéar, C. (2004). Des entreprises aux couleurs de la France. Report to the Prime Minister.

Berger-Douce, S. (2010). Les PME, ces oubliées du management de la diversité ? In *Nouvelles perspectives en management de la diversité*, Barth, I. and Falcoz, C. (eds). EMS, Caen.

Bogaert, S. and Vloeberghs, D. (2005). Differentiated and individualized personnel management: Diversity management in Belgium. *European Management Journal*, 23(4), 483–493.

Boxenbaum, E. (2006). Lost in translation: The making of Danish diversity management. *American Behavioral Scientist*, 49(7), 939–948.

Chemla, P., Fontaine, G., Tetu, V. (2017). La recherche comme accélérateur du pouvoir transformatif des initiatives locales ? Le cas du Pôle Territorial de Coopération Economique TETRIS en Pays de grasse. *Des émergences à la reconnaissance, trajectoires d'innovation*, Montreal.

Deephouse, D.L., Bundy, J., Tost, L.P., Suchman, M.C. (2017). Organizational legitimacy: Six key questions. In *Sage Handbook of Organizational Institutionalism*, Greenwood, C., Lawrence, O., Meyers, R. (eds). Sage, Thousand Oaks.

Desreumaux, A. (2004). Théorie néo-institutionnelle, management stratégique et dynamique des organisations. In *Institutions et Gestion*, Huault, E. (ed.). Vuibert, Paris.

DiMaggio, P. (1988). Interest and agency in institutional theory. In *Institutional Patterns and Organizations: Culture and Environment*, Zucker, L.G. (ed.). Harper and Row, New York.

DiMaggio, P. and Powell, W. (1983). The iron cage revisited: Institutional isomorphism and collective rationality in organizational fields. *American Sociological Review*, 48, 147–160.

Douglas, M. (1986). *How Institutions Think*. Syracuse University Press.

Emirbayer, M. and Mische, A. (1998). What is agency? *American Journal of Sociology*, 103(4), 962–1023.

Garud, R., Jain, S., Kumaraswamy, A. (2002). Institutional entrepreneurship in the sponsorship of common technological standards: The case of sun Microsystems and Java. *Academy of Management Journal*, 45(1), 196–214.

Greenwood, R. and Suddaby, R. (2006). Institutional entrepreneurship in mature fields: The big five accounting firms. *Academy of Management Journal*, 49(1), 27–48.

Kelly, E. and Dobbin, F. (1998). How affirmative action became diversity management: Employer response to antidiscrimination law, 1961 to 1996. *American Behavioral Scientist*, 41(7), 960–984.

Kirton, G., Greene, A.M., Dean, D. (2007). British diversity professionals as change agents – Radicals, tempered radicals or liberal reformers? *International Journal of Human Resource Management*, 18, 1979–1994.

Klarsfeld, A. (2009). The diffusion of diversity management: The case of France. *Scandinavian Journal of Management*, 25(4), 363–373.

Lauring, J. (2013). International diversity management: Global ideals and local responses. *British Journal of Management*, 24(2), 211–224.

Maguire, S., Hardy, C., Lawrence, T.B. (2004). Institutional entrepreneurship in emerging fields: HIV/AIDS treatment advocacy in Canada. *Academy of Management Journal*, 47(5), 657–679.

Meyer, J.W. and Rowan, B. (1977). Institutionalized organizations: Formal structure as myth and ceremony. *American Journal of Sociology*, 340–363.

Pelled, L.H., Eisenhardt, K.M., Xin, K.R. (1999). Exploring the black box: An analysis of work group diversity, conflict and performance. *Administrative Science Quarterly*, 44(1), 1–28.

Perrow, C. (1986). *Complex Organization: A Critical Essay*. McGraw-Hill, New York.

Pfeffer, J. and Salancik, G.R. (1978). *The External Control of Organizations: A Resource Dependence Perspective*. Harper and Row, New York.

Scott, W.R. (1995). *Institutions and Organizations*. Sage, Thousand Oaks.

Seintanidi, M. and Crane, A. (2009). Implementing CSR through partnerships: Understanding the selection, design and institutionalisation of nonprofit–business partnerships. *Journal of Business Ethics*, 85, 413–429.

Sippola, A. and Smale, A. (2007). The global integration of diversity management: A longitudinal case study. *The International Journal of Human Resource Management*, 18(11), 1895–1916.

Süß, S. and Kleiner, M. (2008). Dissemination of diversity management in Germany: A new institutionalist approach. *European Management Journal*, 26(1), 35–47.

Suddaby, R. and Greenwood, R. (2005). Rhetorical strategies of legitimacy. *Administrative Science Quarterly*, 50(1), 35–67.

Tesch, R. (1990). *Qualitative Research: Analysis Types and Software Tools*. The Falmer Press, New York.

Thomas, D. and Ely, R. (1996). Making differences matter: A new paradigm for managing diversity. *Harvard Business Review*, September–October.

Conclusion

Acting for the Enterprise, a Major Societal Challenge in a Context of Worsening Inequalities and Poverty

In this book, the possible role of an enterprise in promoting inclusion in a territory was illustrated using specific initiatives and questioned. More or less recent institutional strategies whose primary aim was not to guarantee better inclusion in the territory can now be associated with this objective. For example, employer groups, which were created to make it easier for SMEs to create jobs, are now making certain areas more attractive thanks to the effects of networks that encourage the pooling of skills. The existence of technology parks also bears witness to this, whose primary objective is to fulfill a technological and entrepreneurial development function for the territory, and which, within the framework of private and public territorial development schemes, provide local residents with access to a form of mobility.

Other entrepreneurial and public mechanisms studied in this work, in contrast, aim at inclusion from the outset. Some are based on developing a particular business status, such as the social enterprise in South Korea. Others are built from a bottom-up perspective through a symbiosis between the enterprise and its territory of establishment. Thus, the entrepreneur not only develops inclusion systems but also ensures intermediation between a

Conclusion written by Martine BRASSEUR, Didier CHABAUD and Pascal GROUIEZ.

diversity of actors in the territory. Local, and also national and even international, partnerships stand out as fundamental. In France, the "Territories with Zero Long-Term Unemployment" system mobilizes existing institutions (the employer State, local systems for regulating competition, etc.) to reduce the number of long-term unemployed in a given territory. In Quebec, there are credit organizations, which develop community inclusion schemes allowing people in financial difficulty to realize their entrepreneurial projects.

Finally, in terms of managing inclusion in an enterprise, some of the work in this book highlights the importance of the need to pay greater attention to this issue in developing corporate culture in order to recognize the richness of diversity for the enterprise. Other work highlights the importance of developing specific institutional arrangements, such as territorially based inclusive recruitment methods.

In all cases, the willingness of top management to support inclusion seems to be a decisive element for the success of such projects. When these projects succeed, they can spread throughout a territory and lead to institutional isomorphisms in corporate management of the problem of inclusion. At the same time, our work has provided an opportunity to examine the role of women, not as beneficiaries but as driving forces in the development of inclusion schemes in a reciprocal relationship with their territory of action.

Throughout the chapters, the initiatives emerged as diverse and as bearers of sustainable social innovation. However, although aiming for inclusion in a territory is not in vain, inclusion remains a particularly worrying issue in all societies. Over the period that this book was prepared, and despite all the initiatives implemented, poverty and inequality have only worsened. Indeed, the pandemic has accentuated social fractures and highlighted the interrelation between the phenomena of discrimination and exclusion, while at the same time making the vulnerability of certain categories of the population even more salient. Thus, the map of social inequalities coincides with that of excess mortality: in Île-de-France, for example, a comparison of the first semesters of 2018, 2019 and 2020 reveals excess mortality in 2020, with the characteristic that, in the most affected geographical areas, inhabitants had the lowest income levels and live in the most cramped housing in the metropolis (Burgel et al. 2020). This bleak geography of disadvantaged locations (neighborhoods, regions or countries) is mirrored internationally. The health crisis has not only highlighted this but has exacerbated income inequalities (Fabre et al. 2020) and increased the proportion of the population in extreme poverty. The relationship with the territory clearly emerges along with the observation both that vulnerabilities are universal and that there is a spatial fragmentation reinforcing the disparities.

This is illustrated by the example of the impact of lockdown on female Canadians. Grekou and Lu (2021), for example, with supporting data from a survey on the labor force (*enquête sur la population active* ((EPA)), point out that, when comparing the period from March 2020 to February 2021 with that from March 2019 to February 2020, "year-to-year job losses were uniformly more severe for women than for men". Other studies, such as those by Nguyen (2020) and Dang et al. (2021), have shown that, on the one hand, permanent employment losses due to Covid-19 affected women more than men in China, Japan, South Korea, Italy, the United Kingdom and the United States and, on the other hand, there has been heterogeneity in exclusion effects across countries. One of the reasons given for this is that, whatever the culture, the burden of domestic tasks and childcare is always placed heavily on women. Another factor relates to the concentration of women's jobs in occupations or sectors of activity that have been strongly impacted by the pandemic. Beyond the existence of a political will to open up society and support gender equality, the resurgence or persistence of women's confinement to the private sphere, with access to the professional sphere still a priority of or reserved for men, highlights the difficulties and limits of inclusion mechanisms.

Generally speaking, the efficiency of the approaches implemented is not guaranteed, and they may have perverse effects that are beyond the control of the stakeholders and independent of their investments. Thus, according to Dang et al. (2021), the phenomenon of "flattening of the world", which can be observed in regions that are similar in their economic and social dynamism and their capacity for innovation, both of which are remote from and connected to international networks, is accompanied by problems of unemployment and the production system becoming obsolete in some neighboring territories. These are the ones that are more specifically confronted with the problem of inclusion and, at the same time, have great difficulty in promoting it. The expression in itself takes on a double meaning. On the one hand, it designates a universe that is certainly developing, but one that normalizes rather than equalizes and that is integrative only within its borders. The health crisis refers us to this paradoxical inseparability that generates both interdependence and division; it is illustrated by Kaplan's (2021) accounts in *L'aplatissement de la terre* (*The Flattening of the Earth*). It also expresses the feeling of powerlessness among inclusion entrepreneurs who, like Zola (1874, p. 56) in *Le Forgeron* (*The Blacksmith*), would have "wanted to flatten the world with a stroke of [the] pen" and are faced with the permanent resurgence of exclusion phenomena and the persistence of discrimination.

Much remains to be done both to understand these phenomena and to act within organizations and in partnerships. This book contributes to opening up inclusion enterprises in territories, both for researchers and to support those responsible for inclusive projects. Of course, it is necessary to extend the perspective, since acting for inclusion requires taking into account the diversity of the population's situations, whether we are talking about factors of disability, illness or even social markers, and, moreover, the company's action is not isolated; mobilizing all the stakeholders in the territory is essential to work for inclusion. The second volume sheds light on these situations in order to better understand how local partnerships are at the heart of an inclusive territory.

References

Burgel, G., Ghirardi, R., Schirrer, M., Burgel, P.R. (2020). Le coronavirus dans le Grand Paris : démographie et société. *Villes en parallèle*, 49(50), 90–119.

Dang, H.A., Delemotte, T., Kramarz, F., Schmutz, B. (2021). *L'emploi et le territoire*. Presses de Science Po, Paris.

Fabre, B., Lallemand, C., Dutronc-Postel, P. (2020). Impact de la crise et des mesures budgétaires 2020–2021 : l'impact sur les ménages. *Conférence annuelle sur l'évaluation du Budget du 16 novembre 2020*. Institut des Politiques Publiques et CEPREMAP, Paris.

Grekou, D. and Lu, Y. (2021). L'emploi et les différences selon le genre un an après le début de la pandémie de COVID-19 : une analyse par secteur d'industrie et taille de l'entreprise. Report, Ottawa [Online]. Available at: https://doi.org/ 10.25318/36280001202100500005-fra.

Kaplan, L. (2021). *L'aplatissement de la terre suivi de Le Monde et son contraire.* P.O.L., Paris.

Nguyen, C.V. (2020). *Gender Inequality During the COVID-19 Pandemic: Income, Expenditure, Savings, and Job Loss.* IZA Institute of Labor Economics, Bonn.

Zola, E. (1874). Nouveaux contes à Ninon [Online]. Available at: https://library.um. edu.mo/ebooks/b31264992.pdf.

List of Authors

Annie BARTOLI
LAREQUOI
Paris-Saclay University
Versailles
France

Amel BEN RHOUMA
CEDAG
Paris Cité University
France

Éric BIDET
ARGUMANS
Le Mans University
France

Martine BRASSEUR
CEDAG
Paris Cité University
France

Didier CHABAUD
Chaire ETI
IAE Paris Sorbonne
France

Rahma CHEKKAR
Laboratoire VALLOREM
University of Orléans
France

Renaud CHENON
ISA Groupe
Aubigny-sur-Nère
France

Pascal GROUIEZ
LADYSS
Paris Cité University
France

Anne JOYEAU
CREM
IGR-IAE Rennes
France

Isabelle KUSTOSZ
CRISS
IAE Valenciennes
France

Sébastien LE GALL
LEGO
Southern Brittany University
Vannes
France

Elena MASCOVA
IRTEM
AFMB
Fontainebleau
France

Douglas MCCABE
McDonough School of Business
University of Georgetown
United States

Stéphane MEURIC
Technopôle Transalley
Valenciennes
France

Paul MULLER
BETA
University of Lorraine
Nancy
France

Gwénaëlle POILPOT-ROCABOY
CREM
IGR-IAE Rennes
France

Gilles ROUET
LAREQUOI
Paris-Saclay University
Versailles
France

Bérangère SZOSTAK
BETA
University of Lorraine
Nancy
France

Delphine WANNENMACHER
CEREFIGE
University of Lorraine
Nancy
France

Index

BRUYÈRE Christelle
Caring Management in Health Organizations: A Lever for Crisis Management (Health and Innovation Set – Volume 3)

HELLER David
Valuation of the Liability Structure by Real Options (Modern Finance, Management Innovation and Economic Growth Set – Volume 5)

MATHIEU Valérie
A Customer-oriented Manager for B2B Services: Principles and Implementation

MORALES Lucía, DZEVER Sam, TAYLOR Robert
Asia-Europe Industrial Connectivity in Times of Crisis (Innovation and Technology Set – Volume 16)

NOËL Florent, SCHMIDT Géraldine
Employability and Industrial Mutations: Between Individual Trajectories and Organizational Strategic Planning (Technological Changes and Human Resources Set – Volume 4)

DE SAINT JULIEN Odile
The Innovation Ecosystem as a Source of Value Creation: A Value Creation Lever for Open Innovation (Diverse and Global Perspectives on Value Creation Set – Volume 4)

SALOFF-COSTE Michel
Innovation Ecosystems: The Future of Civilizations and the Civilization of the Future (Innovation and Technology Set – Volume 14)

VAYRE Emilie
Digitalization of Work: New Spaces and New Working Times (Technological Changes and Human Resources Set – Volume 5)

ZAFEIRIS Konstantinos N, SKIADIS Christos H, DIMOTIKALIS Yannis,
KARAGRIGORIOU Alex, KARAGRIGORIOU-VONTA Christina
*Data Analysis and Related Applications 1: Computational, Algorithmic and
Applied Economic Data Analysis (Big Data, Artificial Intelligence and Data
Analysis Set – Volume 9)*
*Data Analysis and Related Applications 2: Multivariate, Health and
Demographic Data Analysis (Big Data, Artificial Intelligence and Data
Analysis Set – Volume 10)*

2021

ARCADE Jacques
Strategic Engineering (Innovation and Technology Set – Volume 11)

BÉRANGER Jérôme, RIZOULIÈRES Roland
The Digital Revolution in Health (Health and Innovation Set – Volume 2)

BOBILLIER CHAUMON Marc-Eric
*Digital Transformations in the Challenge of Activity and Work:
Understanding and Supporting Technological Changes
(Technological Changes and Human Resources Set – Volume 3)*

BUCLET Nicolas
*Territorial Ecology and Socio-ecological Transition
(Smart Innovation Set – Volume 34)*

DIMOTIKALIS Yannis, KARAGRIGORIOU Alex, PARPOULA Christina,
SKIADIS Christos H
*Applied Modeling Techniques and Data Analysis 1: Computational Data
Analysis Methods and Tools (Big Data, Artificial Intelligence and Data
Analysis Set - Volume 7)*
*Applied Modeling Techniques and Data Analysis 2: Financial,
Demographic, Stochastic and Statistical Models and Methods (Big Data,
Artificial Intelligence and Data Analysis Set – Volume 8)*

DISPAS Christophe, KAYANAKIS Georges, SERVEL Nicolas,
STRIUKOVA Ludmila
*Innovation and Financial Markets
(Innovation between Risk and Reward Set – Volume 7)*

VALLIER Estelle
Innovation in Clusters: Science–Industry Relationships in the Face of
Forced Advancement (Smart Innovation Set – Volume 36)

2020

ACH Yves-Alain, RMADI-SAÏD Sandra
Financial Information and Brand Value: Reflections, Challenges and
Limitations

ANDREOSSO-O'CALLAGHAN Bernadette, DZEVER Sam, JAUSSAUD Jacques,
TAYLOR Robert
Sustainable Development and Energy Transition in Europe and Asia
(Innovation and Technology Set – Volume 9)

BEN SLIMANE Sonia, M'HENNI Hatem
Entrepreneurship and Development: Realities and Future Prospects
(Smart Innovation Set – Volume 30)

CHOUTEAU Marianne, FOREST Joëlle, NGUYEN Céline
Innovation for Society: The P.S.I. Approach
(Smart Innovation Set – Volume 28)

CORON Clotilde
Quantifying Human Resources: Uses and Analysis
(Technological Changes and Human Resources Set – Volume 2)

CORON Clotilde, GILBERT Patrick
Technological Change
(Technological Changes and Human Resources Set – Volume 1)

CERDIN Jean-Luc, PERETTI Jean-Marie
The Success of Apprenticeships: Views of Stakeholders on Training and
Learning (Human Resources Management Set – Volume 3)

DELCHET-COCHET Karen
Circular Economy: From Waste Reduction to Value Creation
(Economic Growth Set – Volume 2)

DIDAY Edwin, GUAN Rong, SAPORTA Gilbert, WANG Huiwen
Advances in Data Science
(Big Data, Artificial Intelligence and Data Analysis Set – Volume 4)

DOS SANTOS PAULINO Victor
Innovation Trends in the Space Industry
(Smart Innovation Set – Volume 25)

GASMI Nacer
*Corporate Innovation Strategies: Corporate Social Responsibility and
Shared Value Creation*
(Smart Innovation Set – Volume 33)

GOGLIN Christian
*Emotions and Values in Equity Crowdfunding Investment Choices 1:
Transdisciplinary Theoretical Approach*

GUILHON Bernard
Venture Capital and the Financing of Innovation
(Innovation Between Risk and Reward Set – Volume 6)

LATOUCHE Pascal
Open Innovation: Human Set-up
(Innovation and Technology Set – Volume 10)

LIMA Marcos
Entrepreneurship and Innovation Education: Frameworks and Tools
(Smart Innovation Set – Volume 32)

MACHADO Carolina, DAVIM J. Paulo
Sustainable Management for Managers and Engineers

MAKRIDES Andreas, KARAGRIGORIOU Alex, SKIADAS Christos H.
*Data Analysis and Applications 3: Computational, Classification, Financial,
Statistical and Stochastic Methods*
(Big Data, Artificial Intelligence and Data Analysis Set – Volume 5)
Data Analysis and Applications 4: Financial Data Analysis and Methods
(Big Data, Artificial Intelligence and Data Analysis Set – Volume 6)

MASSOTTE Pierre, CORSI Patrick
Complex Decision-Making in Economy and Finance

MEUNIER François-Xavier
Dual Innovation Systems: Concepts, Tools and Methods
(Smart Innovation Set – Volume 31)

MICHAUD Thomas
Science Fiction and Innovation Design (Innovation in Engineering and Technology Set – Volume 6)

MONINO Jean-Louis
Data Control: Major Challenge for the Digital Society
(Smart Innovation Set – Volume 29)

MORLAT Clément
Sustainable Productive System: Eco-development versus Sustainable Development (Smart Innovation Set – Volume 26)

SAULAIS Pierre, ERMINE Jean-Louis
Knowledge Management in Innovative Companies 2: Understanding and Deploying a KM Plan within a Learning Organization
(Smart Innovation Set – Volume 27)

2019

AMENDOLA Mario, GAFFARD Jean-Luc
Disorder and Public Concern Around Globalization

BARBAROUX Pierre
Disruptive Technology and Defence Innovation Ecosystems
(Innovation in Engineering and Technology Set – Volume 5)

DOU Henri, JUILLET Alain, CLERC Philippe
Strategic Intelligence for the Future 1: A New Strategic and Operational Approach
Strategic Intelligence for the Future 2: A New Information Function Approach

FRIKHA Azza
Measurement in Marketing: Operationalization of Latent Constructs

SKIADAS Christos H., BOZEMAN James R.
Data Analysis and Applications 1: Clustering and Regression, Modeling-estimating, Forecasting and Data Mining
(Big Data, Artificial Intelligence and Data Analysis Set – Volume 2)
Data Analysis and Applications 2: Utilization of Results in Europe and Other Topics
(Big Data, Artificial Intelligence and Data Analysis Set – Volume 3)

UZUNIDIS Dimitri
Systemic Innovation: Entrepreneurial Strategies and Market Dynamics

VIGEZZI Michel
World Industrialization: Shared Inventions, Competitive Innovations and Social Dynamics
(Smart Innovation Set – Volume 24)

2018

BURKHARDT Kirsten
Private Equity Firms: Their Role in the Formation of Strategic Alliances

CALLENS Stéphane
Creative Globalization
(Smart Innovation Set – Volume 16)

CASADELLA Vanessa
Innovation Systems in Emerging Economies: MINT – Mexico, Indonesia, Nigeria, Turkey
(Smart Innovation Set – Volume 18)

CHOUTEAU Marianne, FOREST Joëlle, NGUYEN Céline
Science, Technology and Innovation Culture
(Innovation in Engineering and Technology Set – Volume 3)

CORLOSQUET-HABART Marine, JANSSEN Jacques
Big Data for Insurance Companies
(Big Data, Artificial Intelligence and Data Analysis Set – Volume 1)

SAMIER Henri
Intuition, Creativity, Innovation

TEMPLE Ludovic, COMPAORÉ SAWADOGO Eveline M.F.W.
Innovation Processes in Agro-Ecological Transitions in Developing Countries
(Innovation in Engineering and Technology Set – Volume 2)

UZUNIDIS Dimitri
Collective Innovation Processes: Principles and Practices
(Innovation in Engineering and Technology Set – Volume 4)

VAN HOOREBEKE Delphine
The Management of Living Beings or Emo-management

2017

AÏT-EL-HADJ Smaïl
The Ongoing Technological System
(Smart Innovation Set – Volume 11)

BAUDRY Marc, DUMONT Béatrice
Patents: Prompting or Restricting Innovation?
(Smart Innovation Set – Volume 12)

BÉRARD Céline, TEYSSIER Christine
Risk Management: Lever for SME Development and Stakeholder Value Creation

CHALENÇON Ludivine
Location Strategies and Value Creation of International Mergers and Acquisitions

CHAUVEL Danièle, BORZILLO Stefano
The Innovative Company: An Ill-defined Object
(Innovation between Risk and Reward Set – Volume 1)

CORSI Patrick
Going Past Limits To Growth

MASSOTTE Pierre
Ethics in Social Networking and Business 1: Theory, Practice and Current Recommendations
Ethics in Social Networking and Business 2: The Future and Changing Paradigms

MASSOTTE Pierre, CORSI Patrick
Smart Decisions in Complex Systems

MEDINA Mercedes, HERRERO Mónica, URGELLÉS Alicia
Current and Emerging Issues in the Audiovisual Industry
(Diverse and Global Perspectives on Value Creation Set – Volume 1)

MICHAUD Thomas
Innovation, Between Science and Science Fiction
(Smart Innovation Set – Volume 10)

PELLÉ Sophie
Business, Innovation and Responsibility
(Responsible Research and Innovation Set – Volume 7)

SAVIGNAC Emmanuelle
The Gamification of Work: The Use of Games in the Workplace

SUGAHARA Satoshi, DAIDJ Nabyla, USHIO Sumitaka
Value Creation in Management Accounting and Strategic Management:
An Integrated Approach
(Diverse and Global Perspectives on Value Creation Set –Volume 2)

UZUNIDIS Dimitri, SAULAIS Pierre
Innovation Engines: Entrepreneurs and Enterprises in a Turbulent World
(Innovation in Engineering and Technology Set – Volume 1)

2016

BARBAROUX Pierre, ATTOUR Amel, SCHENK Eric
Knowledge Management and Innovation
(Smart Innovation Set – Volume 6)

BEN BOUHENI Faten, AMMI Chantal, LEVY Aldo
*Banking Governance, Performance And Risk-Taking: Conventional Banks
Vs Islamic Banks*

BOUTILLIER Sophie, CARRÉ Denis, LEVRATTO Nadine
Entrepreneurial Ecosystems (Smart Innovation Set – Volume 2)

BOUTILLIER Sophie, UZUNIDIS Dimitri
The Entrepreneur (Smart Innovation Set – Volume 8)

BOUVARD Patricia, SUZANNE Hervé
Collective Intelligence Development in Business

GALLAUD Delphine, LAPERCHE Blandine
*Circular Economy, Industrial Ecology and Short Supply Chains
(Smart Innovation Set – Volume 4)*

GUERRIER Claudine
*Security and Privacy in the Digital Era
(Innovation and Technology Set – Volume 1)*

MEGHOUAR Hicham
Corporate Takeover Targets

MONINO Jean-Louis, SEDKAOUI Soraya
*Big Data, Open Data and Data Development
(Smart Innovation Set – Volume 3)*

MOREL Laure, LE ROUX Serge
*Fab Labs: Innovative User
(Smart Innovation Set – Volume 5)*

PICARD Fabienne, TANGUY Corinne
*Innovations and Techno-ecological Transition
(Smart Innovation Set – Volume 7)*

2015

CASADELLA Vanessa, LIU Zeting, DIMITRI Uzunidis
*Innovation Capabilities and Economic Development in Open Economies
(Smart Innovation Set – Volume 1)*

CORSI Patrick, MORIN Dominique
Sequencing Apple's DNA

CORSI Patrick, NEAU Erwan
Innovation Capability Maturity Model

FAIVRE-TAVIGNOT Bénédicte
Social Business and Base of the Pyramid

GODÉ Cécile
Team Coordination in Extreme Environments

MAILLARD Pierre
Competitive Quality and Innovation

MASSOTTE Pierre, CORSI Patrick
Operationalizing Sustainability

MASSOTTE Pierre, CORSI Patrick
Sustainability Calling

2014

DUBÉ Jean, LEGROS Diègo
Spatial Econometrics Using Microdata

LESCA Humbert, LESCA Nicolas
Strategic Decisions and Weak Signals

2013

HABART-CORLOSQUET Marine, JANSSEN Jacques, MANCA Raimondo
VaR Methodology for Non-Gaussian Finance

2012

DAL PONT Jean-Pierre
Process Engineering and Industrial Management

MAILLARD Pierre
Competitive Quality Strategies

POMEROL Jean-Charles
Decision-Making and Action

SZYLAR Christian
UCITS Handbook

2011

LESCA Nicolas
Environmental Scanning and Sustainable Development

LESCA Nicolas, LESCA Humbert
Weak Signals for Strategic Intelligence: Anticipation Tool for Managers

MERCIER-LAURENT Eunika
Innovation Ecosystems

2010

SZYLAR Christian
Risk Management under UCITS III/IV

2009

COHEN Corine
Business Intelligence

ZANINETTI Jean-Marc
Sustainable Development in the USA

2008

CORSI Patrick, DULIEU Mike
The Marketing of Technology Intensive Products and Services

DZEVER Sam, JAUSSAUD Jacques, ANDREOSSO Bernadette
Evolving Corporate Structures and Cultures in Asia: Impact of Globalization

2007

AMMI Chantal
Global Consumer Behavior

2006

BOUGHZALA Imed, ERMINE Jean-Louis
Trends in Enterprise Knowledge Management

CORSI Patrick *et al.*
Innovation Engineering: the Power of Intangible Networks

Printed and bound by CPI Group (UK) Ltd, Croydon, CR0 4YY

23/04/2025

14660909-0002